# BLOCKCHAIN BASICS BIBLE 2022

## The Best Beginner's Guide About Cryptocurrency Technology-Non-Fungible Token (NFTs)-Smart Contracts-Consensus Protocols-Mining-Blockchain Gaming & Crypto Art

# DISCLAIMER
## © Copyright 2022

# Table of contents

# Introduction

The book offers an excellent guide to understanding Blockchain technology for beginners. Those who are unfamiliar with this technology can gain a better understanding of the contents if they avoid technical details. However, some terms will be more understandable if you have some IT background. It isn't necessary, though. It has been written in everyday English to avoid confusion, and it will walk you through the entire process of how digital currency was created step-by-step.

Our goal is to understand what caused the birth of several cryptocurrencies in our current society by going back in time and summarizing the history of finance. We then examine the primary objective behind the invention of Bitcoin as well as the theory behind it. As we move forward, we should review some of the possible candidates for the birth father of blockchain. The next part of our discussion will describe what a distributed ledger is and how it operates. Afterward, the miners are introduced, their responsibilities, and who they are. Then it discusses how the blocks are created, and finally, how the blocks culminate into a chain called a Blockchain.

We will discuss in more detail what security measures we have put in place on the Blockchain in the last chapters. In addition, by examining the purpose of this technology and future banking systems, we will attempt to understand why it will change the world. To conclude, here is a quick explanation of what Blockchain is. It's no doubt that there are many books available on this subject, so thanks for choosing it! I have taken every necessary step to make sure the book is packed with useful information. Have fun!

# A Brief Overview Of Blockchain

I would like to touch on Bitcoin first before explaining what Blockchain is. There's a common misconception that Bitcoin is the same thing as Blockchain. However, that is not the case. Bitcoin and Blockchain aren't the same things. Blockchain-based technology allows and keeps Bitcoin alive, which is a cryptocurrency, digitized money.

The first application on the Blockchain platform to be tested was bitcoin when the platform first appeared. In a sense, Bitcoin could be thought of as Blockchain since it's the first application built on Blockchain technology. Blockchain, however, is not Bitcoin. Let me explain. Despite blockchain's complexity, there are still very few people who know about every aspect of it. Blockchain technology is so complex that human beings are continually finding new issues that this technology can solve. Blockchain is solving problems, as we can see. But it's causing certain problems for some large financial institutions. In the news, you can see that an increasing number of companies are turning to Blockchain technology for various purposes. But, of course, some of these issues are still being addressed.

Blockchain can solve a wide range of problems since not only can it solve one issue for some people, but it can also solve many problems for everyone. Because Blockchain has been running since 2008, it has reimagined the financial institution, and that's why it has been around for nine years already. We can blame or reward no one on the Blockchain, as it is a globally distributed database that is completely decentralized. All computers are affected, and it cannot be stopped. There are multiple blocks in the Blockchain, each of which cannot be replaced. Since it contains multiple blocks, it represents unalterable truth. A new chain is added to the existing Blockchain when it is created, replicating itself on the Blockchain system on the Internet, then synchronizing the same details on all computers running the blockchain. Because of this replication, it is irreplaceable.

As a result, all administration is transparent. Because new chains are created every 10 minutes, you can add and expand without human intervention, which is an efficiency the human mind has never been able to achieve. People of all races, backgrounds, and religions can have full accessibility when a new block becomes visible on every computer in the world.

Blockchain today resembles the internet in 1992-1993 in terms of its position. Many people back then said, "it's nonsense, or it doesn't make sense." Certainly, the internet was young at the beginning, which meant that there were many fewer computers, few websites, and a slow network. Those with power in politics or large retail infrastructure already thought the Internet (interconnected networks) was a dumb idea. They trusted it to be nothing more than background noise. However, the internet grew and developed at an exponential rate. Eventually, local support for the internet became an integral part of it. Do not assume that Blockchain will not have the same effect as traditional technology. In the current state of innovation, technology is advancing fast that humans cannot keep up. Instead of talking about the future, let's look back at finance's past and how Blockchain will change that dramatically.

# Finance In History

This section focuses on understanding our existence through innovation. Let's go back hundreds of years and see what we found out.

As trading is a fundamental component of our food chain, it has always been present in our lives and is likely never to go away. Taking a closer look at the basic human needs for survival, you quickly notice that three major requirements must be fulfilled:

- Water
- Air
- Food

Air and water are easily accessible, so I will take the example of food and analyze it in more depth. Humans have considered food items to be one of the essential components of survival since the earliest times. Food has therefore always been considered crucial. It was one of the first methods humans used to exchange goods or services, and it was part of the global trading chain, like anything else of value. Because food has always played a vital role in basic survival for thousands of years, it was the most lucrative business model. Several locations around the world still use this approach to this day. The evolution of civilization and the development of villages and cities have led to changes in payment methods. At the time, we didn't have freezers or fridges, so food items like exotic fruits and meat just went to waste because there wasn't a place to store them. Several problems arose because of this. This had to be fixed. Our payment method had to not easily decay or waste to solve this problem—the points required to be exchanged for food or other goods and services.

**Precious metal**

The world was introduced to shiny metals as a new payment method, such as silver or gold. The idea was initially unpopular with most people. However, the idea was implemented, and everyone gradually accepted it. Silver and gold were exchangeable for food items and other goods and services, and they are still always increasing in value today as the silver or gold price rises. However, the mining of gold and silver has become much more difficult because of climate change. Consequently, the precious metals have been discontinued as payment currencies.

**Paper money**

It initially seemed ridiculous to introduce paper money, as humans are uncomfortable with change and reluctant to adapt to things we aren't familiar with. However, as time progressed, nearly every country in the world implemented centralized paper money systems. New methods of payment, such as paper money, have taken off all over the world. Paper money is indeed okay, but we can cite countless examples of paper money that has failed due to its value decreasing in the long term. Other factors are responsible for the decline in the value of paper money, such as its ease of counterfeiting on a large scale.

Further, as with anything in the world, we know that goods with limited supply inevitably grow in value, especially over a long period. When paper money is printed repeatedly, however, its value decreases, lowering the purchasing power of the money. Nevertheless, there is something impressive about paper money.

We keep re-inventing new paper money, even though we have learned repeatedly that paper money is flawed. It will, however, be successful this time. Take the euro, for instance, which has replaced currencies like:

- Dutch guilder
- Finnish markka

- German Mark
- French franc
- Greek drachma
- Spanish peseta
- Slovak koruna
- Maltese lira
- Austrian Schilling
- Italian Lira

Paper money will likely remain in use for quite some time. However, another currency known as SWIFT was introduced in our new digital world after the paper form.

## SWIFT

This new company was established in 1973 and allowed all financial institutions to send secure financial transactions across the globe in a safe, reliable environment.

Yet another truly revolutionary idea. It's very convenient to make payments using the internet, and the fact that contactless cards are very convenient these days. The efficiency at which transactions can be processed is quite good. Using your mobile device or your laptop, you can make an international bank transfer wherever you are, within 3-5 days. Initially, people didn't believe it would ever work when it was first introduced, as it seemed alien. However, certain payments have become easier to automate in recent years. For example, paying your bills or subscribing to a service, most large companies now pay all their employees via bank transfers. It's true that many companies still pay their workers cash-in-hand without taking into account taxes. Various reasons exist why these companies choose to remain anonymous and not disclose all of their assets to the banks. People were forced to adapt as always. There was a sense of awe in knowing that all your wealth was contained on one piece of plastic.

A new trend has taken place in the world of payment. Centralized banks have developed their systems, and they now offer many different options for customers to choose from. The most common virtual payment methods include:

- Credit Card
- ATMs
- Visa Debit
- Debit Card

Other digital payment methods were introduced by various third-party companies as a result of the dot-com boom and the internet revolution, allowing investors to enjoy more secure transactions for a fee. Despite being more expensive, we can now make international operations with companies or people we never need to communicate with. The third-party guaranteeing that the payment will only be completed once the goods arrive as described allows us to still complete transactions even if we are unsure about a business or particular goods. PayPal is an example of a payment method you use because you know that you can get a refund, and PayPal will make sure that you are compensated if the goods or services are not as described.

Among the many centralized financial systems that are well known are:

- Alipay
- eCash
- PayPal
- Payoneer
- M-Pesa and much more Digital currency

Several new currencies were introduced in 2008, but this time they were very different. The first was called Bitcoin, and it was a digital currency. However, a well-known company or bank did not introduce it, nor did any government, but rather a software program using a Blockchain protocol.

Most people initially weren't interested in adopting it; they didn't understand its purpose. They may need to do some research to understand it. Many different currencies exist, and we know that cash works. Using our bank cards is an easy way to make a payment, and there are so many other payment options, so why bother? Because Bitcoin was the first digital currency to be introduced.

Nonetheless, as of June 2017, there were more than 730 different types of digital currencies. How do they impact our lives? When I ask my friends who do not work in the IT industry about Bitcoin and cryptocurrency, they often look at me as if I speak a foreign language.

Even though some might have heard of cryptocurrencies, they don't even bother to investigate their potential - and how much they can contribute to our future. In short, when looking back through history and analyzing the history of financial institutions, it is possible to notice that the form of payments has significantly decreased from their physical value. As a result, we are not only seeing these currencies becoming smaller, lighter, or thinner but also becoming more virtualized. Eventually, people won't even have to make them since these digital currencies run on our current internet (interconnected networks).

# Bitcoin Basics

**B**lockchain technology is what runs it, making it the first digital currency. There is no central authority behind it. It cannot be manipulated. You may also know it as digital money or electronic money. The system works by exchanging funds between peers. The system is a computer program. The program has no physical presence since it grows on your computer's hard drive. Indeed, it is present on every computer that exists today.

There is no physical presence of this currency since it only exists in a digital format. Therefore, there does seem to be some fluctuation in its value. It has, however, maintained a strong trend for a long time: in addition, it has steadily increased. For example, it was 0.05 dollars per bitcoin back in 2008 when the dollar started competing. Yet, one bitcoin has touched a record high value of $2,912.00 in June 2017, its highest level to date. In the years since its creation, Bitcoin has demonstrated its ability to reach its peak repeatedly and increased in value above anything we have ever seen with any other form of currency.

According to the currency exchange rate for bitcoin against the dollar for the past ten years, it has continued to grow. As long as bitcoins keep on increasing in value, especially around the four-year mark, I believe that will continue to happen. What makes me think that? You will just have to trust me.

## Do you know how many bitcoins there are?

That's a good question, and you can figure it out yourself. Depending on the date and time, you should read this book at the right time and the right place. Before calculating anything complicated, let's look at some facts we are familiar with. On October 31, 2008, the first 50 bitcoins were created. Every 10 minutes after that, an additional 50 bitcoins were created. By 2016, bitcoin production had been reduced to half - 25 bitcoins were created every ten minutes. As of 2016, the process has followed the same principles, meaning 12.5 bitcoins are created every 10 minutes until 2020. There will be 21 million bitcoins on the market by 2140 when this process is completed.

## Bad reputation

For those unfamiliar with the Dark Web, let me give you a brief overview. The Dark Web is so fascinating that I could write a whole book about it in the future. But I am not attracted to online transactions involving drugs or guns. Just because it is a list of things I can purchase on the Dark Web doesn't mean I will ever purchase anything from there.

In essence, you need to understand that the Internet, in its current form, through search engines like Google, Yahoo, and Bing, isn't the only one out there. TOR, another search engine, allows you to access the darknet, known as the darknet. TOR network is sometimes referred to as onion router or onion network. By hiding the end-user's IP address, TOR makes what they do on the internet untraceable.

The only thing your ISP knows is that you visited the TOR network, regardless of what website you visited. You could explore the site yourself and see what kind of services are available there, but that is entirely up to you. As you browse the dark web, you will encounter ugly services. I have been to the dark web before to get a feel for it. Lastly, I'm sorry to mention these, but I have seen simply disgusting things, and I do not recommend this to those who are easily upset. I am referring to the fact that the gun and drugs traders on Tor accept Bitcoin as a payment method. The TOR network and Bitcoin are untraceable. This makes the Dark Web an ideal hideout for criminals.

Do criminals use Bitcoin as well? You bet they do. When they seek illegal goods or services online, they have little choice but to resort to illegal means. I encourage you to think about using bitcoin because criminals also use it before you close this book. Cryptocurrencies are not intended for criminals. There are 3 billion people worldwide who can be saved with bitcoin when it comes to financing. Bitcoin was designed for everyone, so don't disregard those 3 billion people.

The second problem is that people have their bitcoin wallets emptied due to account hacking. Let me be clear. Rather than bitcoin itself, the hackers compromise end-user computers and mobile devices. The value of bitcoin has gone up immensely, and hackers are also becoming more educated. The hacking of Bitcoin accounts has changed their game, and they have realized that it is profitable and untraceable; therefore, why not do it? There is no need to worry about this issue anymore. If you decide to buy a wallet, just be sure that you always back it up and always have all the security features enabled. Fortunately, some security features like 2-step authentications don't require much time or effort, but it's better to be prepared than to assume that hackers won't find you. People who have lost bitcoin accounts due to hacks have stopped trading or investing in bitcoin and other cryptocurrencies.

## Wikileaks

WikiLeaks is a website where a non-profit organization anonymously publishes secrets and classified information. The website is unpopular with individual governments, and they have ordered the site to be shut down. The site's basic maintenance and security are required, and the only contributors capable of helping do so only using bitcoin. Therefore, the site has been up and running for decades. Among the most famous examples is the American Civil War site. Bitcoin has been used to donate to countless causes people have assisted, even to people on the other side of the planet.

The most popular speculations and accusations against bitcoin revolve around its fluctuating value. Why is it that way? It's often asked, "How about a cryptocurrency that uses the same underlying technology as bitcoin that can compete with it? Can bitcoin's value decrease?" Such accusations may be true, but looking at the history of bitcoin value, only significant increases have been seen, even compared to 734 other cryptocurrencies.

I am not a futurist, but based on the information available, I think it's safe to say that bitcoin is on the rise and will continue to rise for a long time to come.

**What can you buy?**

Although you can purchase anything on the dark web, I am not advising you to do so as you could be in danger of being hacked into or stolen by criminals. It is even possible for criminals to use blackmail on you. Regardless, you shouldn't have to provide your details if you do not provide them. More and more services accept bitcoin, such as Hotels, Restaurants, Coffee shops, even some takeout shops now recognize bitcoin as a payment method.

Shopify, TigerDirect, and many other large retailers accept bitcoin as well. If you look around your area, you will see how wide the range can already be. Some of the things you can find in the big cities include:

- Private Jets
- Theatre
- Taxi Service
- Pubs
- Bicycle rent

As well as these, you might consider other large companies that accept Bitcoin, such as:

- Microsoft
- Zynga
- Wordpress.com
- Alza
- Lionsgate Films
- OK Cupid
- Stream

- Reddit
- Subway
- Del
- Expedia.com
- Virgin Galactic
- Badoo… and many more

In addition to being able to purchase on websites with the help of Gift cards, multiple applications function like gift cards for things like:
- Zappos
- CVS Pharmacy
- Target
- Nike
- Amazon.com
- Walmart
- iTunes
- eBay
- GAP
- BEBE
- Best Buy
- Starbucks
- Sears
- Papa Johns
- The HOME depot… and much more.

It was important that you know some of the largest companies in the world are already accepting bitcoin. The categories that are available in our store can help you to better understand the goods and services we offer to choose from:
- Clothing
- Airline
- Department Stores
- Automotive
- Beauty

- Electronics
- Gas
- Home and Garden
- Grocery
- Gifts and Toys
- Shoes
- Jewelry
- E-Commerce
- Health
- Movies
- Home improvement
- Hotel
- Pets
- Restaurants
- Sporting goods

There are many categories listed, and if you want to know what stores you can buy from with bitcoin, try checking nearby stores or finding out what online platforms will deliver to your area.

## Why do not all people use Bitcoin?

Unfortunately, most people who already know about bitcoins are too lazy to do some research to understand their potential. My first experience with bitcoin was back in 2013, and I didn't give it much thought. I understood that bitcoin is a form of online payment method, and criminals mostly use it due to its untraceable nature. It's just that. The news doesn't mention it very often, apart from the occasional cyberattack where the hackers demand bitcoin to unlock the system.

In any case, at the beginning of this year, I rediscovered bitcoin as I studied Network Security, so I told my buddy Rob about it. According to him, bitcoin had a value of about $300, and he was aware of its existence. It was inconceivable for me to believe that one bitcoin was worth $300 when Rob told me! Bitcoin was something I had never heard of before. It still didn't occur to me that it only exists in digital format. I still thought it was like a real physical coin. Afterward, another friend Viktor, who was overhearing our conversation, asked why I had never heard of bitcoin before! Hence, I said, "Yes, I heard about it, but I didn't realize it was worth that much." I became more interested in it and began to do some research on it. Several days later, I had an idea to make bitcoin with my old laptop! As a result, Viktor and Rob were curious about how computers could generate bitcoins, and I told them that I heard they were worth about $300 each, and I might be able to generate one or two each week. It was clear that I had no idea what I was talking about, and they told me it wasn't that straightforward. It was, however, impossible for them to explain how it's done. According to them, I was thinking like a hacker, and I shouldn't have been thinking like that, as it was for criminals. However, I did say that it sounded like an exciting technology. "So what's the benefit of having bitcoin?" they asked. Interested in something in particular? Are you interested in buying something from the dark web? It left me speechless, so I didn't say anything. Meanwhile, I started learning and acknowledging everything I could about bitcoin, which led me to another fascinating technology known as Blockchain.

It is relevant to note that most people have been misled by fake news, and for those that might be interested, understanding how bitcoin or Blockchain functions takes time. Consequently, most people don't get involved in research and give up before they start.

# The Trigger

When Lehman Brothers collapsed, some of you might recall when everything seemed just fine back then. Then, the largest bankruptcy in US history, the 15th of September 2008, occurred. Lehman Brothers were operating in other countries too, and the outcome of that day was the same wherever it was located.

The time was when I was working in Canary Wharf, London, UK. I was working as an assistant manager in a restaurant called Nando's during those days. Groups of people arrived at our restaurant carrying boxes containing their belongings from the office. Our server informed us that they would not be eating there anymore. We did not understand what these customers were talking about at first because we had been working hard and were isolated from the news.

Our attention was quickly drawn to the news at Canary Wharf, where we discovered that Lehman Brothers UK had been placed in administration (bankruptcy) just 45 minutes earlier. Consequently, we understood and realized that those who used to eat lunch at our restaurant would no longer have the opportunity to come around. A day earlier, 2,000 people had lost their jobs. A total of 2,500 more followed the following day, on the 16th of September. Our management team decided to provide free soft drinks to those who just lost their jobs to demonstrate our sympathy. All of those customers were also lost along with others. I just wanted to share my experience right at the beginning of the recession in 2008 when I was working. The Lehman Brothers bankruptcy led to many more Banks and Financial Institutions choosing administration over bankruptcy protection. News channels were awash with stories about another large company losing all its assets, time and time again. Unemployment rose simultaneously, and then slowly, many people began losing their homes due to unpaid mortgage payments.

Many small businesses needed to close. People were thinking twice before spending money in the restaurant, as there were fewer customers there. It was not just the US and UK that suffered from the financial crash, but many other countries that are still suffering from recessions. During that period, the housing price began to fall and finding a new job was difficult, especially since overqualified individuals applied everywhere. Job openings, however, were not sufficient to meet the growing demand; as a result, the market stagnated.

The news, like most people, is manipulated a great deal and serves only to create fear and drama amongst hard-working people... I am not trying to harm any company's image, but controlling the media is an excellent way to manipulate people, beliefs, and freedom by making people believe that the world is exactly what the media is providing, the use of media such as news channels and newspapers is indeed one of the best methods to create slaves. Just think about the number of people you meet on an average day. A few people, if not most, will tell you a story that begins, "Did you hear the news?" Of course, someone else will follow up with, "Where did you hear that?" The response will be something along the lines of, "I heard it on XYZ news station, or in the news, or read it in the XYZ newspaper." Everything is enormous news for a few days, sometimes weeks, and then it's all forgotten. Why is this so? Surprisingly, around the same time, on an unfrequented internet forum, a document titled Bitcoin was uploaded to a cryptography mailing list on metzdown.com. A Peer-to-Peer Electronic Cash System was the subtitle.

So, what exactly is it? It's not from CNN, the BBC, NBC, CNBC, or any other news station. As a result, it must be gibberish, right? Yeah, it's probably bogus news, and whatever it is, it appears too convoluted. As a result, it piqued no one's curiosity. This white paper was released in October 2008, less than two months after the world's largest financial catastrophe. The author identified himself as Satoshi Nakamoto and outlined a few facts about Bitcoin, new digital money. He added that he felt he had discovered a solution to the world's most pressing problem, a technology known as the blockchain. He also demonstrated how it works and that it has already been developed and is functioning in software form on the existing internet.

There are various opinions about what happened, and you may discover multiple answers regarding what transpired, the most crucial of which is—why now? How could such a significant paper be released so soon after the worst financial catastrophe in history? Of course, we could find out someday soon, but we may never know what sparked the birth of Blockchain technology.

# The Inventor

First and foremost, please realize that this book was written in the second quarter of 2017. Consequently, once you have finished reading this book, fresh light may have been shone on who Satoshi Nakamoto is.

Let's attempt to figure out who Satoshi Nakamoto is based on what we know right now.

First and foremost, Satoshi Nakamoto is the creator of bitcoin as well as blockchain technology. Even though it is a fictitious identity, this is how he announced himself to the internet. It's a boy's name. It is plausible, however, that Satoshi Nakamoto is a woman. This is one of the most perplexing puzzles in the realm of technology. Instead, most people do not want to know who Satoshi is; however, they are grateful for the technology he built. It is a common misconception that Satoshi Nakamoto has owned Bitcoin and blockchain technology since he invented them. The identity of Satoshi Nakamoto is not relevant since he does not control the Blockchain or bitcoin.

But, we still want to know who's behind the curtain, so let's think about it again. Satoshi Nakamoto might be a guy or a woman, a couple, a group of individuals, or even a gaggle of women, for all we know. Satoshi Nakamoto might be a small group of ten persons or a large group of 100 people. Satoshi Nakamoto might be a toddler or an elderly man. Finally, Satoshi Nakamoto may have died shortly after releasing his white paper, leaving him little opportunity to reveal his true identity.

I understand if you're tired of hearing these allegations, so let's start thinking in a new way. Satoshi Nakamoto may not be human at all. You may think of me as having reached my limit.

However, it's strange that we haven't been able to find out who Satoshi Nakamoto is in the last decade; not where he lives, but who he is—honestly

—we have no clue. Someone may be able to identify him. However, no confirmation has ever had enough proof to show who Satoshi is.

I've always enjoyed watching science fiction films, and I recently discovered one called Arrival. Some of these classic films are still relevant today. Back in the day, for example, some science fiction books depicted certain products or technologies that we could use in the future, as well as others that we've been using for years. I don't want to dig into many technicalities but consider facetime back in the 1980s. It was only a thought that one day we might be able to achieve something like that. And nowadays, we use Skype and Facebook Video Chat daily.

Millions of individuals are connected and capable of staying on Skype video chat for hours on end utilizing our cell phones. The original iPhone was developed and released to the public ten years ago, in 2007. We've seen some tremendous developments since then, and the following decade will be even more spectacular.

So, returning to the film Arrival, I hope you've already watched it and that I won't ruin anything for you. If you haven't already watched it, you might want to skip the following few sentences.

In the film, we are visited by Aliens who are come to assist humanity by offering visibility in the future. But, again, if you haven't seen the movie yet, you'll probably despise me for this.

The film's themes are outstanding, so it's no surprise that it got one Oscar, even though it may have deserved more, but that's just my view. When I think about this sci-fi film, I think about its similarity to the same principles. We obtained Blockchain technology from an unknown individual—or, more accurately, from an unknown person.

Our world will shift radically as a result of an anonymous source! I'm curious how the film's makers came up with the idea... I'm not saying there are Aliens out there, but I also can't say there aren't. What I can tell you is that this technology fascinates IT Professionals, Software Developers, Experienced Programmers, and even Cybersecurity Experts, and it is sometimes referred to as an ALIAN TECHNOLOGY."

The blockchain is massive, and it will undoubtedly take months, if not years, to completely comprehend its technical complexities and how it fits into the larger picture.

Another issue is that it is increasingly being claimed that this technology is simply too sophisticated for one man to create. As a result, Satoshi Nakamoto could not have been working on it alone.

So, let us return to the million-dollar question: "Who is Satoshi Nakamoto?" First, let's take a look at some of the claims made over the years so you can make your own decision. You must realize that Satoshi Nakamoto fell silent in 2009 and stayed so for the following five years, at least on the forum where he previously commented and was always active.

**Not a Satoshi**

Satoshi Nakamoto was 41 years old when the Bitcoin white paper was published, according to legend. He is Japanese. However, the initial code produced for the blockchain was written in English, and it would be impossible for a Japanese individual to write like that. It would imply that he hired or was working with someone who speaks flawless English to create the code.

In 2014, a few newspapers began to publish about Dorian Nakamoto, who was living in the United States in California at the time. Satoshi was Dorian's given name at birth. Furthermore, additional facts might lend credence to his claim to be the true inventor of Blockchain.

Apparently, the first reporter who attempted to contact him asked him, via email, if he had anything to do with bitcoin.

Dorian's reaction was, "I am no longer involved with that, and I cannot address it." It has been delegated to others. They are now in command of everything. "I'm no longer connected." That, of course, raised suspicions, and reporters descended on Dorian's home in California. He read his e-mail again after understanding how serious it was and tried to explain himself.

First and foremost, he has denied any affiliation with bitcoin. In fact, he stated that he had no idea what bitcoin was until his son informed him of the news, at which point he checked it up on the internet. He also went public and stated, "I have nothing to do with bitcoin." It has nothing to do with development. I was merely an engineer doing something else at the time. If you look at the time spent in 2001, you'll notice that I wasn't there. I was employed by the government through a contracting firm. I only think the fictional name was inserted by mistake."

There have also been revealed papers indicating that he has been conducting classified work for the US Government as well as the US Military. He has also signed agreements stating that he would not be able to disclose any role in his prior efforts with secret projects.

Following this occurrence, an unexpected message appeared on a P2P forum where the Real Satoshi Nakamoto used to post after five years of silence. "I am not Dorian Nakamoto," he says.

Craig Wright, a well-known Australian businessman, emerged in 2015 as the next probable candidate to be Satoshi Nakamoto.

Documents regarding Craig Wright had begun to leak to Wired magazine from an unnamed source. However, the majority of them provided proof that suggested Craig Wright was Satoshi himself.

Craig has mentioned that he is considering releasing a Cryptocurrency paper in one of them, issued in August 2008. This, of course, became a highly appealing contender for Satoshi Nakamoto's first white paper, which was published in October 2008, barely a month later.

Another leak, this time from Wired magazine, was another statement by Craig Wright, but this time from January 2009. He wrote this time that bitcoin is set to go live. The very first bitcoin transaction took place in January 2009.

Wired magazine also reported that they had received several e-mails and transcripts confirming the relationship. "A leaked correspondence from Wright to his lawyer from June 2008 shows Wright imagining a peer-to-peer distributed ledger."

There were several leaks about Craig Wright, particularly in Wired magazine. In May of 2016, though, everything changed. On his blog, Craig Wright said that he is now prepared to confess that he is Satoshi Nakamoto openly.

This was another watershed moment, although many people remained skeptical. Craig posted on his blog two days later that he would finally share a series of posts to establish the groundwork for his astonishing claim. Craig has changed that post with the following instead of presenting evidence:

"I'm sorry." I was sure that I could pull it off. I felt like I could leave my years of obscurity and hide behind me. But as this week's events developed and I prepared to reveal the proof of access to the early keys, I broke. I'm lacking in bravery. I am unable to.

When the rumors started, my credentials and character were attacked. Then, when those charges were found to be untrue, fresh claims arose.

I am aware that this flaw will cause significant harm to individuals who have it.

Jon Matonis and Gavin Andersen, in particular, helped me. I am only able to hope my acts do not permanently tarnish their honor and credibility.

They were not duped, but I know the rest of the world would never accept it.

I can only apologize.

"And good-by."

Craig has been labeled a liar by the bitcoin community since he has not offered any proof that he is the genuine Satoshi.

Craig then performed yet another spectacular motion. He requested an interview with the BBC. He then revealed his identity as Satoshi Nakamoto, the inventor of bitcoin. Craig further indicated that he would not take any trophy or award for this innovation since he is not interested in money or anything else from anyone, and he surely does not need anyone's support.

When the reporter asked him why he had been hiding for so long and how he had only now revealed himself, he had a relatively straightforward explanation.

Craig stated that he did not choose to approach the cameras since he has individuals that selected this for him; yet, he is unhappy with the current scenario because it will damage many of his friends and family and his staff members.

The interviewer then asked him what he wanted from the notion of being the founder of Bitcoin, but he responded that he didn't want anything, only to keep working on his projects. Craig said that just because he developed bitcoin or publicly published a paper for free to benefit people, it does not mean that he is obligated to do so in the future.

That doesn't mean he should become a well-known celebrity, and no one should push him to reveal what projects he's working on. Then he went on to say that he was the driving force behind the invention of Bitcoin. He did, however, require assistance in finishing it.

The reporter then said something that most people are interested in. As the creator of bitcoin, Craig must own 5% of every bitcoin preserved, which is a substantial sum of money. The value of bitcoin decreases whenever traders sell bitcoin for dollars. However, because the creator owns so much of it, there is concern that if the designer sells all of it when the price is high, the bitcoin would most likely fluctuate.

So the reporter proceeded to question him how much bitcoin he possessed and how much he had deployed thus far. Craig just responded that it doesn't matter how many he has; rather, what matters is when he would deploy them. Craig then concluded his statement by saying that he understands that some people will believe him while others will not, but he doesn't care because he will never be on camera.

The truth is that Craig is quite compelling, and I'm at a loss for words. I won't pass judgment on him or Dorian, but the environment we live in is certainly odd. Consider that for a moment. We anticipate someone who denies any connection, but when we locate a man who admits to being him, we don't believe him. Doesn't it sound like we'll never find out whom the actual Satoshi is?

Craig has shown how he initiated the very first bitcoin transaction. But he only let one person view it, and that was a reporter with no technical background. The average techie is not convinced. Craig has stated that he has never wished to be photographed. Still, now that he's done it—proven he's the genuine Satoshi—he needs to back it up with proof that he conducted the first bitcoin transaction, and he has many options for how to do it. One proper method is to have someone, such as a bitcoin specialist, look at it and confirm that he is not lying. His approach is a little phony because no one can guarantee that he is who he claims to be 100 percent of the time.

So, what exactly is the objective of all of this? Some have speculated that if Craig assumed the title of Satoshi, the actual Satoshi would send a message in some way allowing him to be located. However, unlike Dorian, there has been no more communication from the genuine Satoshi.

Consider this: if you were one of the world's wealthiest men in secret, what would you do?

Would you go to the BBC and broadcast this to the entire world? Speaking to the World not only makes Craig popular among ordinary people, but it also puts him at risk of being attacked by cybercriminals and black hat hackers immediately soon. It's so basic that anyone could grasp it right away. So, when you think of someone brilliant enough to develop a technology that will change, if not already has changed the world, don't you think of hackers?

As previously stated, most IT professionals are not convinced, so the question of which the real Satoshi Nakamoto is remained unanswered.

Some believe Craig was the genius behind blockchain technology, while others believe Dorian was the genius. Nevertheless, most bitcoin community members are skeptical that they have anything to do with bitcoin or blockchain. There are numerous other possibilities as well, and I am going to explain a few of them.

**Nick Szabo**

According to sure researchers, a significant theory is that Nick Szabo writes the bitcoin white paper. In comparison to more than ten possible people involved in bitcoin's creation, Szabo's published writings were the closest linguistically to Satoshi Nakamoto's original white paper.

In addition to being a computer scientist, Nick Szabo is also an expert cryptographer and expert in Bitcoin. Furthermore, he is renowned for his talks on Blockchain technology, digital currencies, and smart contracts.

These themes pique the curiosity of many individuals—particularly well-known speakers on the subject of Blockchain or bitcoin. However, few people know what some of these so-called specialists were up to before Bitcoin's inception. In 1998, Nick Szabo came up with the concept of "Bit

Gold," decentralized digital money. Isn't it a strange coincidence? Nick had the concept, but he also devised a mechanism for Bit Gold and subsequently built it. Nick did not update his weblog daily. In reality, he had a reputation for not publishing anything; but, when bitcoin was launched in 2008—just two months after its formal release—Nick began to write more extensively about Bit Gold. There isn't a lot of information on him. It isn't much known about him. An excellent example is that Nick's birth date has not even been verified by anyone yet; as a result, other curious individuals have begun to dig deeper into Nick.

Nick Szabo was listed on Wikipedia as a law professor at George Washington University; however, the University had no record of anyone by that name. In other words, this has given rise to the possibility that Nick Szabo is not even his real name but instead his pen name.

Since Nick does not have a verified age, education, location, or even previous work career, there is no evidence to prove that he is the father of bitcoin; therefore, he is the top candidate within the technology world.

Whenever he has been questioned if he has anything to do with Bitcoin, he has reportedly always denied it, and he has been silent for a long now. Unfortunately, there is so much bogus, made-up news in the media that it's almost incredible. The internet was the sole legitimate source of news at the beginning of the twenty-first century; however, now that most publications have migrated online, it takes a great amount of effort to discover the truth. That is to say, most people who are constantly looking for the truth, and I am referring to IT professionals who just study technology, do not read newspapers or false news channels. When a technological invention is announced, such as the blockchain, these nerds become obsessed with finding out who exactly created it, and they begin to research until they find out the truth. The consensus among tech gurus appears to be that Nick Szabo is the real creator of bitcoin.

Previously, I mentioned that there are many assumptions about possible candidates for the father of Blockchain technology. Of course, the answer will vary depending on who you ask; however, I wanted to introduce some of the main characters who may have had some role in creating bitcoin.

## Teamwork

Due to its complexity, there is a general belief that blockchain may have involved many characters rather than one specific individual. When asked about it, Craig said that he had some help. However, the main person in charge was him. Therefore, many have begun to believe it may not be Craig, but rather Satoshi Nakamoto, who represents a group of individuals rather than an individual's name.

Japanese names for the three words are Satoshi, Naka, and Moto. Satoshi means clear thinking or wisdom, and Naka means inside. It is possible to combine these three words in many different ways. One of the most common is when the team, or the individual, says something like: I understand this system completely from the inside out. You could substitute us instead of I. But Blockchain is no accident. For this technology to be created, we needed clear thinking, the ability to fully understand every aspect of it, and finally, Blockchain is a large foundation.

Because of the Blockchain's structure, the opposite thinkers are confident that one person conceived the idea. Therefore, having a team of people think together, creating something similar, would not be as in-depth. For example, rather than the average techie, I am talking about a group of people who have been working on the internet since its infancy and are software developers. As another example, Nick Szabo comes to mind, not a wealthy Australian or an older Japanese who hasn't been involved in anything for a long time.

As we close this chapter, I leave it to your imagination to decide who Satoshi Nakamoto is. Yet, as I mentioned earlier, it may all depend on the date when the book was read; but for now, nearly a decade after the invention of Blockchain technology, we still have no proof that Satoshi is 100% who he claims to be.

# Blockchain-Based Distributed Ledger

This is a handbook for newcomers. As a result, I will try my best to describe the ledger system in as few technical terms as possible. First, consider the ledger system as a family tree; however, instead of names, the massive ledger system stores information about payment amounts and addresses. The ledger stores all payment records dating back to the first transaction ever made in terms of dollar amounts. There are no URLs or geographical addresses when it comes to the addresses. Instead, they are bitcoin addresses or addresses for any other cryptocurrency. The ledger keeps track of all cryptocurrency transactions.

In addition, the current values of prior transfers are constantly calculated. The value allocated to each transaction is represented by one portion of the ledger, while other sections of the ledger represent the date and time of each transaction. This is a lot like any of the current banking systems.

You can see who transferred to which account, when, and how much each transaction cost; nevertheless, there is no banker in the ledger. Furthermore, the addresses do not represent the identities of the persons, nor do they indicate who owns what.

As a result, this might be referred to as an anonymous ledger system. You should know that the bank has the authority to take an individual's bank account if he or she has no relatives.

In addition to banks, any government agency, including the police, FBI, or other government agency, can seize any bank account if they identify a valid reason. The only individual who has access to a bitcoin account within the vast ledger is the person who holds the password to that account.

Of course, it's risky; if you forget the password to your bitcoin wallet, the ledger's value will be lost forever. If you forget your password for your bank account, you contact the bank, they ask you security questions, and you confirm that you are the account owner; the bank will give you access. However, if you have a bitcoin account, no bank will assist you in accessing it. Because the ledger is entirely decentralized, anyone can see it.

As a result, everyone may view your bitcoin account, as well as the amount of value in that wallet. No one, however, can determine that account is linked to you.

Because of blockchain technology, every transaction is validated and placed in a block; each block joins the previously validated blocks. Eventually, they all create a blockchain chain. Every bitcoin citizen is required to preserve a copy of the blockchain, and after each block that the system creates, each blockchain member receives a finished sealed block.

The system then automatically verifies each block and assigns each block to each citizen. This is how blockchain stores every transaction and value ever made. Without the necessity for a central authority, these solutions assure the authenticity and rectification of every transaction.

If all of this seems unfamiliar to you, keep in mind that the system handles everything for you, and you, as a bitcoin citizen, don't have to conduct any calculations yourself, which would take a long time anyway.

The miners are in charge of sealing each transaction into the ledger once it has been validated. Each new verified block must be added to each citizen's blockchain; however, before accepting a new block, everyone must examine the logical continuation of all the values in the new block to ensure that all the cost transfers are legal. This also prohibits hackers or individuals with evil intentions from replicating transfers or counterfeiting them.

Attempting to steal bitcoin or any other cryptocurrency is against the law. This is an important step since the validation will be stored indefinitely in the vast ledger and the blockchain.

For the competition, hashes are used, as well as to validate each block and ensure that each citizen receives the same record.

I hope I didn't mislead you by including details about how the ledger is distributed and its procedure to validate each transaction. The fact is that each validation step is technically accomplished by combining different processes. You should also be aware that thousands of procedures are performed every second. As a result, I've tried to stay away from the technicalities as much as possible.

# Miners

Let's begin by considering how new value enters the system. Satoshi Nakamoto merely produced 50,000 bitcoins to begin the process in 2008. If he had created all 21 million in the first place, the bitcoin would have been worthless, and the concept would have been ridiculous. Satoshi, on the other hand, began by creating a small quantity of bitcoin.

However, as the bitcoin community expands, more value will be necessary to keep the system alive. Therefore, a certain method is required to maintain the system; Satoshi has devised a solution by defining a position. This method addresses not one but two issues: 1. Validating transactions continuously 2. Adding fresh value to a system that already exists Miner is the name of the character.

Individuals or any bitcoin citizen can be miners. However, several huge firms have emerged over time, such as Genesis Mining, where you may join and hire their mining facilities as an individual. In addition, many other miners have formed pools throughout the years, and many of them offer to join these pools for a variety of reasons that I will detail momentarily.

Let me first explain why they are known as miners and what they do. They are. As the analogy with gold or any other valuable metal has been exploited, they are referred to as miners. They collaborate to produce a new value, just like gold miners do when they dig underground. Bitcoin miners, on the other hand, record each transaction on the ledger. As a result, we may refer to miners, finalizers, or authenticators as miners, finalizers, or authenticators.

Miners are paid with bitcoins in exchange for their efforts, and this is how new value is generated to the system. The miners use specific methods to check, authenticate, certify, and finish the transactions. The transaction record cannot be updated after the miners have generated a new block approved by the citizens, making it permanent information. This, too, will be irrevocable. As a result, no individual will ever be able to contest it or amend it in the future.

The miners encrypt the blocks, which requires a significant amount of computational power, ensuring that they cannot be simply copied. Validating processes may be done in a variety of ways, depending on the miner. Some miners may utilize different software or even create their in-house software to speed up the authentication process. It makes no difference what program they use because all of their work will be scrutinized. It begins when a miner begins to collect transactions that have been broadcasted on the network, then checks those transactions before sealing those collections of transfers and operations into a new block. A miner is awarded bitcoins for each sealed block added to the network.

# Creation Of Blocks

Each block creation can be explained in many ways; however, some may seem very confusing, but you also need to consider your level of technical knowledge. The first time you hear it or read it may be challenging. In previous explanations, we have seen that miners have a unique role in verifying each transaction as a block. This time, let's see how blocks are generated.

1. A new block will be created. Although they may only be halfway through validating a block, the miners will eventually give up and focus on starting a new block.

2. New transactions can be selected. There are thousands of operations broadcast across the network, and miners get to choose from them.

3. Check the priority of the transaction. This time, the miners can go back to number one by starting a new block if they find that the previously selected transaction is not that significant. On the other hand, the miners may continue to the next step if the priority is high.

4. Verify the validity of the transaction. Again, there is no exception for any miner to omit this step; it is a process that all miners must follow. Should the transaction be found to be false or invalid, the miners will have to stop the process and go back to number 1, where they will begin a new block and hopefully obtain another valid transaction.

5. The transaction should be accepted. Valid transactions must be accepted if they were tested previously.

6. Transact securely. The transaction must now be sealed if it has been verified as valid and accepted.

7. Within the block, add the transaction to the transaction tree. Once the previous steps have been verified, add the transaction to the

transaction tree.

8. Determine how much each transaction is worth. For a block to be sealed, miners must ensure that there are enough transactions in the transaction tree. In the case of insufficient transactions, the miner will not secure the block until there are enough transactions. Therefore, the miners must add new transactions until there are enough for the block to be sealed until they go back to the number 2 process again and again.

9. Interruptions should be checked. To complete this process, the miner must ensure that no other miners have sealed the block since they with the same transaction inside.

10. The block must be sealed. As soon as the miners receive enough transactions to be sealed, the block will be sealed.

11. You should broadcast the block. During sealing the new block, the miners must broadcast the newly sealed block; if they are interrupted, they may have to start a new block from scratch.

12. The new block should be started. However, the next step in this process is back to step number one, as you can see. During the process of sealing the block, miners might get interrupted, and once the block has been broadcast, if another miner with the same transactions has already sealed another block, the block cannot be accepted. Rather, it must be started from scratch.

It takes about ten minutes for each block to be created. This results in 144 blocks being created every day. As I mentioned before, the miners who have successfully added a new block into a blockchain get rewarded a degree of bitcoin. For example, between 2008 and 2012, each new block would be rewarded with 50 bitcoins. Every four years, the reward for a new block is halved; therefore, from 2012 through 2016, the reward for a new block was 25 bitcoins.

A miner currently receives 12.5 bitcoins for adding a new block to the blockchain since 2016, but that will change to 6.25 bitcoins from 2020 until 2024. Until the last bitcoin is generated in 2140, this process will continue.

# Security On The Blockchain

S ome of you might say, "blockchain is a cutting-edge technology that will positively impact the globe." But, "Is it secure?" remains the question.

Yes, to put it briefly. But first, consider what the system has already accomplished. The truth is that whatever is connected to the Internet, or connected to a system with a web connection, can be hacked and corrupted.

Even if a gadget does not use a connection, it can still be hacked if you have physical access to it. One example is a laptop or desktop computer that can be broken into and launched with a Linux disc. Take banks, for example, if you want to go further.

They are constantly compromised; of course, they have ceased announcing these types of instances because they would lose all of their patrons if they did. In late 2015, a teenager hacked the head of the FBI, and most people find it amusing. Even though the FBI's security is very highly organized, it is nevertheless vulnerable to hacking. Even Kevin Mitnick hacked the FBI for three years and listened to the agents' phone conversations while talking about himself, so the FBI might not be the ideal example to use. When it comes to the NSA or National Security Agency, you've probably heard about Edward Snowden.

Snowden, who stormed out with classified documents, demonstrates that even the NSA has flaws. Confidential documents or even secrets can be leaked.

All of those high-priced firewalls, intrusion prevention systems, and intrusion detection systems are useless unless they are properly upgraded. You must also realize that having all that security means nothing if someone with social engineering skills figures out the password to any of those devices. The consequence would be dramatic, as they often are, but most of the world's largest financial institutions have ceased talking to news outlets about being hacked, fearing that it would harm their reputation and cause shame.

Because firms keep all of their data centralized, hackers only need to target a single company to infiltrate its systems; this is why hackers know that everything can be hacked. It simply takes time and careful planning to break into any system; however, time and careful planning are required when it comes to a system like a blockchain.

It's extremely unlikely. Although experts say it is not impossible, it would still necessitate a massive amount of computing power. Furthermore, blockchain is not protected by firewalls or any other detection or prevention system. Instead, the power of blockchain stems from the fact that it is completely decentralized. What I mean is straightforward. I will be that as it may, do my best to explain it in plain English.

Because blockchain is an open-source technology, the software can be run by anyone. Therefore, you have the option of never purchasing bitcoins or investing in any cryptocurrency. You could, however, become a member of the blockchain community by running the blockchain software. The software is cost-free to download and use, and you will be under no obligation to anyone, but if you decide to run it, you will simply become a blockchain community member.

Your device will become a part of the blockchain once you become a member, and each time a new block is formed, your device will receive a record of the transaction.

Because your gadget has now become a part of the blockchain, more devices should be hacked to completely breach the chain. Your device is now contributing to the existing decentralized system because it is running blockchain software. There are no centralized copies, and each user has the same level of trust as the others. I am saying that there is no master node because every device has the same mirrored data, making hacking almost impossible. The blockchain has been in use for almost a decade and has never been breached.

It's exciting because the blockchain offers an anonymous jackpot of $7 billion to anyone who can hack the system. For years, numerous black hat hackers and huge criminal organizations, and cybergangs have targeted blockchain because of its high price.

Still, blockchain has never been hacked, nor has it ever experienced any form of slowness. This demonstrates that the essential functions have been well-structured; yet, as I previously stated, anything can be hacked; it is only a matter of time. IT experts usually feel that everything is possible in the future with the rapid advancement of technology. The method by which the blockchain system can be attacked is defined by quantum technology. It would, however, necessitate compromising the millions of machines that already run the blockchain software.

Furthermore, to be effective, the hacking of all those devices would have to be done very rapidly. Even if we don't know who Satoshi is or what he's capable of, one thing is certain: he created the system. As a result, he would have access to the first block he produced, allowing him to influence the blockchain system if desired. Multiple blockchain technologies have emerged throughout time, and the value of bitcoin has increased; individuals have also begun to invest enormous sums of money in numerous cryptocurrencies. As a result, people have lost interest in who Satoshi Nakamoto is, or he has simply been forgotten over the years; but, if he or she is still alive and desires to manipulate the system, it is feasible, though I'm not convinced that the conclusion would be in the best interests of the majority.

# Business Purposes

There are many nerds in the technology world, including me. Some people, on the other hand, are not alike. So, to you, how do I define a geek? Because there are so many different geeks out there, so I'll start with the nice ones.

Video games have altered the world, and many young people and adults have gotten infatuated with their favorite titles. However, those who have never spent an entire night or day, or both, playing online games may find it difficult to comprehend why some individuals become addicted to video games.

There are those geeks who only play games and spend money on them, but there are others. Part geeks are preoccupied with new tools and software, believing that they must be checked out as soon as possible, even if some of this software is illegally acquired from torrent sites.

On the other hand, other geeks would not necessarily download everything for free, preferring to buy the original software or tools to feel better about owning the actual thing. Genuine software gives a better feeling, and many geeks buy it out of respect for the authors who contribute to the software.

## Designers and developers

When it comes to blockchain, several new companies have lately emerged that are developing a protocol that will allow certain online games to be played using their in-house developed coin. To top it off, they've designed fantastic online games in which players can participate in their cryptocurrency by contributing CPU or GPU power from their Game PCs, PlayStations, X-Boxes, and other devices. Because these methods would be fully utilized and contributed regularly, their worth would skyrocket.

As you can see, blockchain would allow the creation of a new coin and an online gaming community based on blockchain technology. I used gaming as an example. Many industries, such as music on demand, movies on demand, social networking sites, and so on, are now similarly using blockchain technology.

The introduction of smart contracts, such as Ethereum, is one of the most significant blockchain-based technologies to date. There is a slew of different blockchains out there right now, and each will have an impact on our future at some point. There are many decentralized crowdfunding, healthcare, supply chain, blogging sites, and real-time sharing options, to name a few, but the most significant of them is IoT.

IoT, often known as the Internet of Things, for blockchain has grown quickly in recent years. In recent years, the use of IoT, also known as the Internet of Things, for blockchain has grown rapidly. The Internet of Things is also known as smart devices, connected devices, physical devices, or driverless vehicles. The goal of these devices is to connect to the network and begin sharing data. Automating daily life is a small-scale business involving software, electronics, and sensors that communicate. However, when it happens to large-scale projects, such as virtual power plants, smart homes, intelligent transportation, or even smart cities that can operate using blockchain technology, that's where big money is. Large-scale business plans for big boys necessitate years of planning; however, the technology to enable it now exists.

These initiatives would allow for direct real-world integration into computer-based systems, increasing efficiency, accuracy, and economic advantage while eliminating human participation.

Machine-to-machine (M2M) connections are already in use. However, blockchain will improve this further by speeding up virtualizations and encrypting data into blocks, allowing us to make good use of our data.

# The Future Of Banking

Over the past few years, thousands of banks have emerged all over the world. The present banking system will not disappear tomorrow. At least two decades will be required. However, there is already technology to use alternatives to banks; all that needs to be done is apply blockchain technology by all our vendors, employees, and employers. This is not difficult to accomplish. Nevertheless, most of us are very familiar with the current system, so it may take a while to adopt a new one.

## Gold

When gold was phased out as a currency and replaced with paper money, it took a long time to implement and for everyone to comprehend that wages are now paid in paper rather than gold. As previously said, gold is still a viable payment option in most countries; nevertheless, it is not accepted everywhere.

When you go to the local grocery, you will not pay with gold; however, other establishments may accept it. You can't pay in gold the same way you can't pay in gold when you buy something online, and there are other reasons besides the fact that it's an old-fashioned approach.

Let's take a look at gold's flexibility first. Assume you want to go to the neighborhood coffee shop for a cappuccino. The prospect of paying in gold for a coffee is intimidating.

How would you break or cut the appropriate amount of gold for the business owner, aside from what if you make a larger cut than you intended? The point is that no precious metal can be widely used as a payment mechanism. It's heavy, and cutting or breaking it into the requisite number of pieces is tough;

hence, using it for money in the future is just not feasible.

**Cash**

Unfortunately, paper money, or currency, is constantly being printed. As a result, determining how much is available on the market is impossible. The more it is printed, the less valuable it becomes. We know from history that there is so much money being printed after a period that it eventually loses its value. Inflation becomes the primary concern, and many people become impoverished due to the loss of all their savings in the bank. As a result, governments are forced to manufacture new paper money for the so-called new economy.

The problem is that this system has repeatedly failed spectacularly, and as a result, we all know it's useless. The issue is that governments and banks centralize this system, and ordinary people have little recourse. Digital currency, on the other hand, is unstoppable and, like bitcoin, has the potential to drastically alter the present system.

Another problem with paper money is that it is extremely easy to forge. Every day, innumerable occurrences involving various types of paper money occur. It makes no difference how beautifully paper money is produced; it can be copied. As a result, counterfeiting will always exist. Cryptocurrency, on the other hand, is impossible to forge, copy, or counterfeit.

Keeping in mind that blockchain signifies trust and the precise quantity of digital money, you must comprehend that cryptocurrencies may soon surpass any paper money, especially if it is centralized.

Yes, it is correct! However, there will only ever be twenty-one million bitcoins generated. So, how can there be enough to go around? Each bitcoin, on the other hand, contains 100 million Satoshis. I'm not very strong at arithmetic, so I used a calculator to figure out how many Satoshi will ever be created, and the answer is 2,100,000,000,000,000.

There are about 8 billion people on the planet. So I divided the enormous figure by 8 billion to see how many Satoshis each individual on the planet might have distributed evenly. I came up with the following figure: 262,500.

The reality is that 60% of the population will never have more than $20,000.00 saved in their lifetime; but, before you conclude that this is the result, consider this. Each Satoshi can be divided into other fractions using blockchain technology, such as another 100 million pieces. If that isn't enough, those fractions can be further divided into another 100 million of even smaller sections, and so on. That said, I hope you recognize that Bitcoin has the potential to supply the entire world with a new currency. However, there are already a plethora of different currencies, and institutions have begun to consider developing their digital currencies.

## Ripple

Making international transactions with Swift is currently a headache. It could take 3-5 working days instead of a few seconds like bitcoin and other cryptocurrencies.

Not to mention costs, it will take too long for money to be transferred, and particular countries might not use it. In addition to being super-fast, making payments with several cryptocurrencies that use blockchain platforms have very low costs, if at all. Bitcoin wallets are also available online for anyone to use.

Everyone - meaning everyone. You have to meet the criteria that the bank asks for when you open a new bank account. Some requirements may include having a valid address, being 18 years old, having proof from your employer of your employment and wages, etc. You can open a bitcoin account without any of the criteria mentioned above if you have a smartphone instead of all these headaches. You can even begin making international transactions in a few seconds.

As you can see, the existing problem is that if I want to buy something from you, I have to transfer money from my bank to your bank via PayPal, which will then pay you. To make a payment, at least one additional so-called trustworthy third party is required. The blockchain, on the other hand, would validate that transaction for us. As a result, we would no longer need banks or other trustworthy third parties. All that is required is a few minutes of internet connection.

You must realize that over 2 billion individuals do not have a bank account for various reasons. For example, they may not be qualified, and they may not even be dressed appropriately to enter a bank. Of course, individuals might simply refuse to open a bank account, but the majority of people just live too far away from a bank. As a result, they have opted against having one. They may have access to the internet from time to time. Thus this may serve as their bank, right? So what's to stop you? It would be quite useful to them, and many individuals are currently doing so.

The banks have recognized that creating their cryptocurrency would be a smart idea so that if blockchain takes over the globe, they will be ready for the great boom. Ripple Network was founded in 2012 as a new currency exchange protocol using Ripples as its currency. It may be exchanged for traditional fiat currencies, including US dollars, euros, British pounds, and most cryptocurrencies and commodities. Ripple has made impressive progress in terms of market capitalization by demonstrating that it is a solid investment for traders. After Bitcoin and Ethereum, Ripple is the third biggest cryptocurrency as of June 2017.

Several significant institutions already use Ripple, and this revolutionary payment protocol ensures nearly no costs for any international money transfer. I strongly suggest you conduct your homework before investing in Ripple. The problem is that ripple is a centralized system. As a result, it provides better protection for your ripple account; however, it is a different story when it comes to potential future development. Because the banks have already gained control of ripple, they may alter their value at any time; thus, it is up to you to decide how much and for how long you wish to support the banks.

# Bitcoin Mining: The Basics

Because this book will focus in-depth on the knowledge and nitty-gritty elements that people don't like to talk about, I'll assume you have a basic understanding of blockchain. When it comes to blockchain, as with any other existing technology, only a few people are interested in learning how it works. As a result, I'd like to congratulate you on your decision to pursue your passion further. The majority of individuals are merely interested in listening to music and never learn how to operate a CD player. There are, of course, new ways to listen to music or audiobooks. Nonetheless, this is one of my all-time favorite examples, which I've always used when I'm about to explain anything to someone who isn't interested in what I'm about to say.

The truth is that you don't need to know how a CD player works, nor how music is wirelessly transported to your speakers utilizing Bluetooth technology. This is fine; but, each time you learn a new word, you are forming a new brain cell, raising your IQ, and, as a result, becoming more clever. You will also diminish your risk of losing all of your brain cells. It has been discovered that once a person reaches the age of 30-40, brain cells begin to die, physically disappearing, and there is little that can be done about it. The average human loses 5-10% of his brain power every decade; however, this varies depending on various factors. However, the global average is 7%. Whatever happens, brain cells will die.

However, you may continue to grow new brain cells by learning new words and talents or anything novel to your brain. It's also been proven that learning a new language may boost your IQ by generating many new brain cells.

What is this new language? You may start studying German, Italian, or French. However, when it comes to technology, there are many more languages to learn: C+, C++, Python, SQL, JAVA, Pascal, PHP, and hundreds more. Every minute of your curiosity and study will set you apart from the pack.

This book will concentrate on Blockchain technology. Although it is relatively new, a deeper examination reveals that the underlying technologies that allow the blockchain to function have existed in the past. I'll go through each of these technologies in great detail.

I will also go into great depth about each of these technologies; certain new protocols must be covered in the next chapters due to Blockchain's developments.

Overall, you must recognize that blockchain and bitcoin are not synonymous. The blockchain is a technology that saw its first implementation on the Bitcoin network. Blockchain is what Bitcoin is. However, Bitcoin is merely a cryptocurrency that may be used to replace fiat currencies. Nonetheless, not everyone will appreciate the notion at first.

The blockchain has solved an issue that we have always had: trust. By utilizing blockchain technology, we can eliminate relying on trustworthy third-party services. As a result, any payment or exchange through the internet will be limited to two people.

This is revolutionary because we can widen the trust gap. As a result, the futures market will be faster and cheaper and free of restrictions based on age, ethnicity, sex, occupation, nationality, or anything else.

To preserve all entries that have ever been registered on the blockchain, blockchain uses a distributed ledger system. In addition, proof of work is used to back up the records (more on this later).

Miners have a key role as well, and the two most critical challenges they must address are:

1. Validating transactions continuously

## 2. Adding fresh value to a system that already exists

Individuals or any Bitcoin citizen can be miners, but, over time, several major corporations have emerged, such as Genesis Mining, where you can join and rent their mining facilities as a person.

Many other miners have established pools over the years, and many offer to join these pools.

The miners encrypt the blocks, which takes a lot of computational power and ensures they can't be simply copied. Validating processes may be done in a variety of ways, depending on the miner. Some miners may utilize different software to speed up the authentication process or even create their in-house software. It makes no difference what program they use because all of their work will be verified. The process begins when a miner collects transactions that have been broadcast on the network, checks them, and finally seals the collections of transfers and activities into a new block.

For each sealed block added to the network, a miner is rewarded with Bitcoin. Every 10 minutes, a new block is constructed. As a result, each day, 144 blocks are made. As previously stated, miners that successfully add a new block to a blockchain are rewarded with a Bitcoin degree.

From 2008 through 2012, the prize for creating a new block was 50 bitcoins. Every four years, the prize for a new block is half; thus, from 2012 to 2016, the award for each new block was 25 bitcoins.

Since 2016, the reward to a miner for adding a new block to the blockchain has been 12.5 Bitcoins; however, starting in 2020, it will be just 12.5 Bitcoins. 6.25 bitcoins are available until 2024. After that, this process will continue until the final bitcoin is minted in 2140.

# Peer-To-Peer Network

To keep the blockchain running requires an organization that lives on the web. Besides, inside the organization, there are sure trades for motivations behind refreshes. These updates are needed to consistently keep the appropriated record framework fully informed regarding the most recent square. Assuming you turn your PC on and begin to run blockchain convention on it, it will turn out to be important for the blockchain network. Then, I would do likewise with my PC, and then, at that point, my machine would turn out to be essential for the organization as well. Every gadget associated with the web, and running blockchain, turns out to be important for the organization. This way, many gadgets can speak with one another utilizing the web and continue to refresh one another. Since there is no expert hub or a brought together a machine that has an unexpected reason compared to most, this organization is called a peer-peer organization. Shared organizations have existed for quite a while. Accordingly, nothing is surprising with regards to it. In any case, since it has no expert hub of any sort, this is anything but a unified organization, yet a decentralized P2P organization. This is vital, as it lets you know that there is no manager of any sort; thus, it diminishes the likelihood that at least one hub on the organization could possibly control the remainder of the hubs. Control of any sort is just inconceivably, and that, in itself, is evidence we can trust the framework. This isn't all, obviously, yet the actual organization is exclusively founded on an innovation that existed beforehand; nonetheless, it has an alternate reason this time. You need to comprehend that there is no focal server or focal customer with regard to a distributed organization. In conventional brought together organizations, there are the essential server or focal servers and numerous customers. How they are associated is that the servers are continually directing what the customers can have. Shared organizations, then again, are unique, as all hubs on the organization fill the two needs; they are generally servers just as customers. This means nobody machine can have a greater choice power than some other on a similar organization. Along these lines, P2P networks are continually cooperating, settling on choices together, and similarly disseminating those to all hubs on the organization.

One more issue with concentrated organizations is that one hub is prepared to impart the furthest down-the-line news to the remainder of the organization. First, it would need to send the traffic to the expert hub or server, which then, at that point, would have the choice to do numerous things. The server could control the traffic before sending it to some other hub. Dealing with the traffic would be kind with the server hub, as when the server would get the traffic from customer A, the server would not send similar traffic back to customer A (as that was the source in any case). All things being equal, the server would send the traffic to the remainder of the customers, however assuming this exchange would be controlled now, neither the rest of the hubs nor customer A could ever look into it. Another issue would likewise be on the off chance that the server would choose to send the traffic just for a specific gathering of customers, rather than every one of them. Once more, this could decrease the force of a broadly shared organization, and on account of the blockchain, this would not be a benefit. The more regrettable that could occur in a unified organization is this. When the waiter gets traffic for discussion, information about the most recent affirmed block, envisioning that the waiter would choose not to impart this information to another customer. This would just make the blockchain bankrupt. In this way, the framework's main way would work to utilize a decentralized P2P organization. If you can't help thinking about how the server would settle on such a choice itself, indeed, it would not. Even though controlling a server, or a little gathering of servers, might be direct for an individual, with regards to a P2P organization, an individual with detestable expectations, such as hacking purposes, or traffic controls, would struggle to do as such and the explanation is clear. Managing a huge gathering of machines physically that life all around the web is almost unthinkable. This is the motivation behind assuming you need to open an organization and be the chief; you would make a conventional incorporated organization by having an expert hub that you can oversee whenever you need. Once more, P2P networks have no chief. Hence, there is nobody to a fault, and each machine in the organization has a similar obligation.

**Timing**

In any framework, brought together or not, there is in every case some postponement. This is called inactivity. When one gadget arrives at the other, it's simply never a similar measure of time. Dormancy is the time characterized while the information goes between its source and last objective. This is the sort of thing you might consider understanding, as information spread can take some time, particularly when there are many hubs on a decentralized framework.

We should take a gander at a model for better arrangement. Envision that hub An is prepared to impart its most recent square to hub B, C, and D. P2P networks are otherwise called moronic organizations, as they have no clue about what sort of information they are moving; all they know is once there is information that necessities to get moved across the organization they will do a transmission ensuring that all hubs are getting similar information. So back to our illustration of four hubs and their information proliferation. Envision that hub An is situated in Los Angeles, US; hub B is situated in Sydney, Australia; hub C is in Cape Town, South Africa; and hub D is in London,

UK.

They will all get similar information; in any case, a portion of the hubs might get the information sooner than different hubs. Along these lines, the request for the exchanges may vary on the hubs.

In outline, distributed organizations are useful for the accompanying reasons:

- Reducing overhead by not sharing information over different hubs instead of keeping everything in one brought-together area.
- Reducing the hazard of duplicating and controlling information.
- Reducing outsider obstruction; subsequently, every exchange of shrewd agreements has fewer charges too quicker execution.

# Hashing

This is another point that the vast majority simply skip if conceivable, and I can't fault them. Cryptography has intricacy that not by and large everybody dreams of finding out about. There is a wide selection of sorts of cryptography that exist; notwithstanding, I will attempt to give a valiant effort to save it straightforward for you to comprehend.

There have been exemplary cryptography utilized since the old occasions by the Greeks and Romans, even in Egypt; nonetheless, our center is current cryptography, particularly the one identified with PCs. Before I drag you into it any more profound, let me elaborate on some fundamental terms that are crucial to comprehend before plunging into Cryptography.

## Hash

Hashing is alluded to a decent estimated series of numbers, for instance, 128, 256, 512, 1024, 2048 numbers. Hashing can be performed on documents like text, pictures, sound records, video records, or even programming. It creates an extraordinary hash dependent on that specific record. A singular document goes through a hash toward one side; then, at that point, it comes out mixed on the opposite end. It doesn't make any variation what sort of document you give it a shot on; the outcome is unique. For instance, you may attempt to put an md5 hash in "blockchain." The hash would not be quite the same as "blockchain1."

Fundamentally, MD5 has taken over MD4 hashing.

Allow me to show you the amount of a distinction there is between two fundamentally the same as words. As I referenced "blockchain," I will perform and create an md5 hash on it. Alright, so the md5 hash an incentive for "blockchain" is: 5510a843bc1b7acb9507a5f71de51b98

In any case, presently, I will play out the equivalent md5 hashing on "blockchain1." Let's see the outcome: 1150228f14788047028d774b7c83c5a6

As you see, this is something else entirely; this is because the word is unique, albeit the same; it is as yet an alternate md5 hashing esteem. How about we attempt to do this now with a number, and for effortlessness, I will utilize not very many figures so you will perceive how incredible hashing can be. This time I will perform md5 hashing on a number line of 123, and afterward 124, and check whether there is any distinction. How about we start, will we? Alright, so I have performed md5 hashing on the number string: 123, and the hashing esteem is this: 202cb962ac59075b964b07152d234b70

Presently I will do the equivalent md5 hashing on the number string 124: C8ffe9a587b126f152ed3d89a146b445

The nearest model I can give you is fingerprints or DNS. Those are likewise interesting, and no two individuals have a similar DNS or a similar unique mark. Hashing has been broadly carried out, fundamentally utilized by programming designers. One of the principal reasons is ensuring that the product isn't altered or adulterated while downloading it. I had an issue before when I redesigned a Cisco Switch with another code, which has gone into Romon mode since I was too numb to even consider checking the md5 hash worth of the product. Fortunately, I was doing it inside a testing climate and not underway organization; nonetheless, it made incredible torment and lost hours recuperate the change to its past design. For my situation, I downloaded the code from the right source; in any case, it was by all accounts that our Proxy server is more likely than not ruined midway. Assuming I would have checked the md5 hashing worth of the new code, I would have been more effective at the errand.

MD5 hashing is brilliant; in any case, it isn't called cryptography or encoding. MD5 was carried out first in 1992, and assuming you believe it's a little old, then, at that point, you are correct. MD5 has been compromised a few times because of its weaknesses; alone, it isn't adequate to give the best security. That being said, we should continue to what Cryptography is.

# Cryptography

Cryptography is a cycle characterized by information being changed over into a specific structure, so it is simply accessible to those for whom it was initially planned. In any case, changing over information is difficult to reach to an unapproved end client.

## Encryption:

What the course of encryption does is straightforward. It changes specific information into a structure that is muddled. The encoded information has another normal name: Ciphertext.

## Decryption:

The course of unscrambling is liable for changing over the confusing information back into its unique structure to become more decipherable. For instance, a basic decoded text, after decryption, would turn into plain text. Whenever information has been encrypted and shipped off the objective of the beneficiary, various ways can be utilized for information decoding. There are two predominant procedures to scramble and decode information, one is utilizing Symmetric keys, and the other is utilizing Asymmetric Keys.

## Symmetric Key:

Utilizing symmetric keys is simple. While scrambling, too decoding, we just utilize the equivalent keys. A model here would be an entryway. When you move out to the store, you lock your entryway utilizing your key, and when you get back from the store, you will utilize a similar key to open your entryway, right? Perhaps I am off-base; ordinarily, a similar key is utilized for those reasons.

The symmetric key calculation is exceptionally quick, indeed, multiple times quicker than utilizing Hilter kilter keys. When we were discussing symmetric keys, the same keys are likewise called shared insider facts. As you can see, the issue here is that both the sender and the collector should utilize a same key for both encryption and decoding. This isn't a benefit regarding security, and the blockchain is surely not utilizing Symmetric key calculations. I needed to present some of the nuts and bolts before we jumped into more profundity, like uneven key calculations.

**Deviated Keys:**

Blockchain utilizes Asymmetric key calculations as a component of different calculations it employs. Accordingly, this theme is the thing that you may have been hanging tight for.

To carry out Asymmetric key calculation requires having two distinctive keys. One of them is designated "Public," and the other is classified "Private" key. The justification behind having two keys is basic. One of the keys will be liable for encoding data to turn into a code text, and the other is to unscramble the data to turn out to be plain text. The private key would be produced by the originator, the person who might encode the data, and this private key should be kept mystery consistently. Nonetheless, the public key would be accessible to anybody, which is why it's known as the public key.

The hilter kilter key calculation is much slower than asymmetric key calculation; in any case, the security is more mind-boggling. In this manner, it is more enthusiastically to be hacked. Public and private keys are numerically interconnected, implying that every open key has just one comparing private key. There are hardly any calculations like that. Notwithstanding, blockchain is accurately utilizing the one called: Elliptic Curve Digital Signature Algorithm.

The present circumstance is somewhat unique for how Symmetric key calculation functions. When the private key has been utilized for encoding the data to turn into a code text, it is important to utilize the public key to decode the data back to plain text. Then again, this cycle can be exchanged and utilized a contrary way as well. For instance, I would encode the data utilizing the public key; then, at that point, I would unscramble the mixed text back to plain text utilizing the private key.

Regarding a legal agreement, the conventional method for carrying on with work is that the two players, the purchaser and the dealer, need to sign the agreement, among numerous different reports for authorization. This conventional method of marking contracts is completed with penmanship utilizing a pen. Nevertheless, there are multiple ways of confirming specific reports, and one of the most known is utilizing advanced marks.

Advanced marks are the same as standard conventional penmanship marks. Be that as it may, they are significantly more secure. Regarding penmanship marks, a long history of them effectively is being faked by a master or anybody with little practice. Computerized marks have conquered the issues of fake marks by utilizing some straightforward strategies. The advanced mark gives the beneficiary interesting data; like this, it gives realness.


**Uprightness:** This ensures that while the message was on the way, it had no adjustment or alteration.

**Verification:** This is to give the validness of the sender.

**Non-disavowal:** This is, so the sender can't reject that the message was at any point sent.


If you're thinking about how the advanced mark is made, also checked, let me start by clarifying it. Envision that you need to make a record by adding a computerized mark so anybody would realize that it has a place with you.

What you can do first is to hash the information. Then, you can utilize a private key to encode your information. That is it, as the encoded hash is your advanced mark. Taking this further to demonstrate that it is without a doubt your advanced mark, you need to send the report to somebody who would then be able to unscramble your information. When you send your message to your companion, you additionally need to convey the computerized signature alongside the report. When your companion has gotten the report, the person in question ought to decode your record by utilizing your public key. This time the aftereffect of the hash worth of the report would be HASH1.

Thus, if your companion applied a similar hash calculation on the got report, the consequence of the hash esteem on the got data would be HASH2. Then, your companion should think about the two hashes: HASH1 and HASH2. Assuming the qualities are very similar, it would be verification that your record had no adjustment on the way, the report is begun from you, and it is undoubtedly yours. The present computerized world requests more adaptable and responsive arrangements, then, at that point, manually written marks. Rather than with nothing to do by utilizing customary marks carefully, you can deal with contracts surprisingly fast.

Utilizing advanced marks—arrangements can be shut in minutes—not weeks. Bunches of programming in a real sense allow you to make advanced marks right away. You should choose a record on your PC, right snap, then, at that point, pick utilizing carefully, set your secret word on it and send it off by email.

The cycle is paperless, and the advanced mark is similarly legitimate as the one made without ink. Besides, utilizing a PC and a better approach for utilizing portable applications, by having a versatile ID, you can sign reports and make bank moves utilizing your cell, as it were. This likewise implies that you can be anyplace on the planet, and in seconds you can approve bank exchanges, also marking any records. In reality, research has shown that utilizing advanced marks helps a normal individual save one entire seven-day stretch of extra energy consistently. You might utilize this time as a get-away. Be that as it may, there are different advantages as well—for example, paper. We can save huge loads of paper throughout the planet utilizing advanced marks.

## Logarithm rudiments

Allow me to ask you what do you think the thing that matters is between the number: 0.0000000159, and the number:

0.00000000159? Indeed, assuming you feel torment in your mind as of now relax, it's normal. Logarithms are assisting us with managing little numbers; be that as it may, at times, enormous numbers. This prompts the idea of logarithms. On a very basic level, what logarithms are about is to sort out what power you need to raise and get another number?

Logarithms are one more part of blockchain innovation that is returning in history to the seventeenth century. This revelation has given another capacity that has stretched out past the extent of logarithmic strategies. Logarithms were freely reported in 1614, and it started to improve on troublesome estimations that added to the development of science, too, reviewing and divine routes. In those days, they had made diverse logarithm tables for different estimations; be that as it may, these days in software engineering, logarithms exist. How about we start with a straightforward model for better agreement on how logarithms work.

To have two to the force of three that implies twice two.

$2^3 = 2 \times 2 \times 2 = 8$

In this model, we have three numbers to work with.

$2 >$ this is our base number

$3 >$ this is known as the type that will decide the occasions when the base number should be increased.

$8 >$ this number is known as the item.

Presently envision that the type x is obscure, for this situation $2^x = 8$, so we need to discover what amount is the x, well we realize that in light of the above model; in any case, some of the time it tends to be parcel's messier than this basic model. Assuming you are just inspired by the type, the numerical documentation: $x = \log2\ (8)$

The articulation for the previously mentioned is: $x = \log$ base 2 of 8

Exponentials $x = 2^3$ and logarithms $x = \log2\ (8)$ are each other's contrary energies

The objective of exponentials is to compute the item: $x = 2^3$

The motivation behind logarithm is to work out the example: $x = \log2\ (8) = (8 = 2^x)$

In this way, we wanted a mathematical method that is simply one way yet hard the other way. At the point when the generator has raised two distinct parts, the arrangement appropriates consistently nonstop. Assuming that we raise any base number to any example x, the arrangement is similarly prone to be any number between zero and 17. Notwithstanding, the converse system is difficult. For instance, having the item number and you need to observe the type is difficult to do. This is known as the discrete logarithm issue. Presently we have our single direction work that is not difficult to perform yet difficult to switch. It is experimentation truly, yet assuming you need to know how hard it tends to be, then, at that point, try to keep your hat on. Indeed, having little numbers, this is not difficult to pick apart; nonetheless, assuming we utilize a superb modulus that is many digits long, it becomes unfeasible to tackle. Regardless of whether you approach all calculation power on Earth, it can require millennia to go through all prospects.

# Diffie-Hellman Key Exchange

However long we know, individuals have, without exception, needed to keep quiet. It has required some investment and work to achieve this. As I referenced previously, the utilization of scrambled information can trace back to the days of yore.

In 1976 Whitfield Diffie, along with Martin Hellman, distributed a paper that disclosed how to make public-key cryptography. They depicted a method of utilizing open channels to trade a mysterious key by utilizing a single direction work called a discrete logarithm.

As you can envision, the most serious cryptography issue is to trade the keys between two gatherings. Of course, we would prefer not to set up a typical key. However, we need to do it so that any individual paying attention to the correspondence between the two gatherings doesn't discover the key.

## The issue

Envision that Alice and Bob need to trade the keys; in any case, Eve is paying attention to their correspondence and captures the key sent among Alice and Bob. Lamentably, in case of Eve gets the key, she can encode the information; in this manner, that key would not be tied down enough for Alice and Bob to convey safely.

## The arrangement

To begin with, Alice and Bob would concur openly on a superb modulus and the generator. We should take a model utilizing a Generator of 3 and a great modulus of 17. Then, at that point, Alice chooses a private irregular number, say 15, and works out 3 to the force of 15 mod 17 that would be equivalent to 6. Then, at that point, Alice would send this outcome openly to Bob. Next, Bob chooses his private irregular number, say 13, and works out 3 to the force of 13, mod 17 that would equivalent to 12. Then, at that point, Bob would send this outcome openly to Alice.

Assuming you are still with me, you may have understood that Eve may have caught both freely submitted numbers that are 6 and 12; nonetheless, she would not realize how to manage those figures so she could continue snooping to the discussion among Alice and Bob.

What occurs next is Alice takes Bob's public outcome and raises it to the force of her private number to acquire the common mystery, which for this situation is 10.

Sway takes Alice's public outcome and raises it to the force of his private number, prompting a similar common mystery.

They have done estimation likewise, even though it doesn't seem like it from the beginning. Think about the accompanying:

Alice has gotten the number 12 from Bob, was determined as 3 to the force of 13 mod 17, so her computation was as old as to the force of 13, to the force of 15 mod 17.

Simultaneously, Bob did this: He got the number 6 from Alice, and he determined as 3 to the force of 15 mod 17. So fundamentally, Bob's estimation was as old as' which is 3 to the force of 15, 13. They have done estimation likewise, and the main distinction is that they have utilized the types in an alternate request. The two of them have determined 3 to the force of their private numbers. Eve would not have the option to find the arrangement since she would stall out on a discrete logarithm issue, and with enormous enough numbers, for all intents and purposes unthinkable for her to break the encryption in a sufficient sensible opportunity. This is the way the key trade issue is addressed with no interference at all. Once more, because of Diffie and Hellman.

## Elliptic Curve Cryptography

First, you need to comprehend that Elliptic Curve Cryptography is more than some other advanced cryptography capacities.

In the same way as other cryptographic frameworks, elliptic bend cryptography acquired its power in math. For the most part, the elliptic bend's structure is the accompanying: $Y2 = X3 + AX+B$

An and B are consistent qualities as a rule can be genuine numbers or levelheaded numbers. Elliptic bends should be possible utilizing standard variable-based math; however, they require definitions for expansion and duplication. To see how Elliptic Curve Cryptography functions along these lines, you should first see how Addition and augmentation function.

## Expansion

Envision a bend that you are going to add two focuses to one called A, one more called B. Whenever you have added those two focuses, and you need to define a boundary between them.

Notwithstanding, you might understand that there is a third crossing point on the chart when you do that. Whenever you have tracked down the third crossing point, you should start to draw another line, and this new line, where it catches the bend once more, will turn into your third point that you should call C.

If it's not too much trouble, note C is equivalent to A + B

C=A+B

Then, you can characterize the transitional situation on the top portion of the bend, which you can call X

This is vital because the Addition requires a third block point; notwithstanding, adding two vertical focuses is an indistinct strategy.

Accordingly, this outcome to what in particular is known as the Elliptic Identity, otherwise called Infinity. The justification for this is the point at which you would attempt to add two vertical focuses, there could never be the third capture, and you can't characterize that option.

Then, consider adding another highlight itself:

Assuming that you are adding a highlight, there is no subsequent perspective to be thought of, and you can't define a boundary between them. But, all things being equal, you can define the boundary through A and find where that would block on the bend.

Whenever you have done that, it is a similar system as before by defining an upward boundary, where the line captured the bend, and the crosses will Find point B. Note, B now equals A + A

This is otherwise called Point Doubling. This is without a doubt a typical method for accomplishing numerous events. This is additionally basically the same as another calculation called square to different calculations. On the off chance that you over and over point twofold, you are doing what's viewed as augmentation concerning elliptic bends.

We should call this 2A and continue to contemplate consider the possibility that we need to ascertain 3A. To play out some increase with multiple times A, you need to perform point multiplying multiple times, which means adding A to itself multiple times.

To begin with, you need to define the boundary among 2A and A, and any place that line blocks the bend, you flip across the x as you have done beforehand. As should be apparent, there are loads of bouncing around on the diagram, even to play out a couple of duplications. This calculation is the same as the square duplicate calculation. This is where Elliptic Curve Cryptography gets it straight as it's infeasible to isolate the duplications and find a specific point that you increased dissimilar to in normal variable-based math.

For instance, assuming you've been given the number 10, and somebody says he increased 5 to give you the number 10, you would realize that the other number from the duplication would be 2. In any case, it doesn't work like that in Elliptic bends. This is otherwise called the elliptic bend discrete logarithm issue. To process the multiplier point, you would have to work out every one of the products of the given point until you would observe the one that matches. This is preposterous, particularly when you utilize bigger qualities; because of the calculation intricacy of this issue.

If it is not too much trouble, to comprehend that clarifying completely what Elliptic Curve Algorithm is could take a full book itself, truth be told, books. Notwithstanding, I have attempted to clarify an overall outline about this sort of cryptography as Bitcoin utilizes it, also Blockchain innovation. Momentarily, Elliptic Curve Cryptography is quite possibly the most gotten cryptographic system utilized today. However, it's computationally infeasible to work out the private keys when utilizing the Elliptic bend key trade.

**Checksum**

Some ID numbers have digits installed inside their numbers. A portion of these is not able to the general population, for example, financial balance numbers. These digits can be quantities of characters called Checksum Digits and are utilized for mistake location on the off chance that you mistype the recognizable proof numbers.

We should take a gander at a British ledger number, for instance:

GB29 NWBK 6016 1331 9268 19

In this model, the two-digit checksum esteems are 29. There is an extraordinary calculation applied to this ledger number to work out this checksum esteem. For instance, assuming that you would mistype this record number by composing:

GB29 NWBK 6016 1331 2968 19

Any British bank application will see that this is a mistake because the checksum worth of this number doesn't relate to the normal checksum digit of 92, all things considered, 29.

The majority of cryptographic kinds of money, like Bitcoin, are likewise utilizing checksum digits. To be reasonable, there are so many blockchain executions that it's difficult to say if all cryptographic forms of money are utilizing checksum digits; notwithstanding, with regards to Bitcoin, it is sure. What you need to comprehend is that checksum and hashing are not equivalents; truth be told, there are some huge contrasts between them, so let me clarify them now:

The checksum is intended to identify inadvertent mistakes in little squares of information, such as government-managed retirement numbers, ledger numbers, cryptographic money addresses, etc. Yet, they are frequently extremely quick to figure.
While a hash diminishes huge information to a more modest number in a way that limits the shot at mishaps.

Government-backed retirement numbers or even ledger numbers are just distinguishing proof numbers and have no different capacities, yet recognizing people for Social Security or banking. Nonetheless, the public key has a relating private key that is numerically connected. These keys are utilized to exchange at least two gatherings by utilizing encryption and decoding of information utilizing these keys. The haphazardly produced private key and the determined public key are changed over into private and public locations. There are numerous justifications for why general society and private key pair are transformed into various looking public and private locations, so we should check out a portion of those models:

• Implement checksum digits in addresses to recognize mistyping of the addresses.

- Perform adaptation numbers in addresses to separate between comparable blockchain executions or the climate.
- Apply Base-58 encoding to addresses to stay away from mistyping of the addresses.
- Use the hash calculation to address to decrease the location sizes.

**Vanity addresses**

A vanity address is a public location where the location holder picks the piece of the location. Fundamentally, Bitcoin tends to that have a custom prefix inside. So, to more readily comprehend, how about we investigate a bitcoin address.

1555JSudJlo9HYPLMbbriwoYdFQawszx6SBgIndkshhe

Here the vanity numbers are 555; nonetheless, you can't begin your Bitcoin address with similar numbers as every Bitcoin address consistently begins with the number 1 as the main prefix. Nonetheless, you may decide to have your vanity letters toward the finish of your location, similar to the model beneath:

1JSudJlo9HYPLMbbriwoYdFQawszx6SBgIndkshheCAR

To create vanity tends to yourself; there are numerous stages that you can do; in any case, there are not many things to note here.

Assuming you need to have vanity letters or numbers between one or three characters in length, those locations can be created rapidly. Notwithstanding, assuming you decide to have a vanity address at least four people long, the strategy could take as long as hours or even days to create. It isn't important to make a vanity address; as it may, I will give a few justifications for why you may decide to utilize a vanity address.

Branding: Vanity locations can be great for associations, also further developing memorability for organizations.

Business model: You may decide to utilize some location as an administration for dealing with your customers. For instance, utilizing the word: CarHire inside your location would stick out, causing customers to perceive your business as more expert than a normal vehicle employ administration.

Donation purposes: Again, same as utilizing for business name or administrations. Assuming you need to utilize a Bitcoin address for gift purposes, you might decide to mirror that inside your location, which would be noticeable to the individuals who move to it.

Just the public key (a bitcoin address) is custom when the vanity address is created. The private key would stay arbitrary. In principle, the whole location can be custom; be that as it may, it is infeasible to produce a location with the prefix of more than 6 or 7 characters.

A few sites will make vanity addresses for you; in any case, don't utilize any of them except if they utilize split-key age joined. This capacity is where they would create a public and private key pair, and you would give them the public key. Then, they would make a vanity address with your public key, also another key pair. Utilizing this method, the help that would make another vanity address would just know a portion of the private key expected to utilize Bitcoin. If they don't utilize this method, then, at that point, it is conceivable that those administrations would have the option to take any Bitcoin put away on that location.

A few issues concerning vanity tend to that are great to know. For instance, as I referenced, anybody can make a vanity address, which is great. Nonetheless, programmers—or anybody with terrible expectations—may likewise realize that reality and attempt to utilize it for their potential benefit. For example, what a dark cap programmer would do is straightforward truly: they could utilize your genuine organization or gift name inside their Bitcoin address and attempt to get assets by imitating you or any business that means well. Another disadvantage, once more, is that more drawn-out prefixes could consume a large chunk of the day to produce.

**Blockchain is cash.**

Indeed, blockchain isn't by and large cash; in any case, when you contemplate what cash is true, I am certain that you need to consider cautiously to reply. Indeed, there are basic answers, and characterizing what cash is, utilizing a single word, what strikes a chord is this: installment.

Cash is a kind of installment in return for help or a singular item. Since you realize that cash is some sort of installment, we should contemplate the worth. Certain items have various qualities in various nations; to isolate limits and measure the upsides of every item to various nations, a few guidelines can be bought and whatnot everywhere. Blockchain has no restrictions: it's running on top of the web, which is open from any place on the planet.

Notwithstanding, with regards to electronic installments, there are issues, and a major one is twofold spending. Back in the mid 80's e-cash was imagined as a mysterious cryptographic electronic cash. How it worked, in an improved on clarification, is this:

Banks made electronic cash that was cryptographically marked. The computerized cash contained a novel ID, otherwise called a token. Clients had the option to buy these assets, then, at that point, start to spend them in shops. What happened was that e-cash depended on an outsider to get approval or some sort of verification, that the e-cash was substantial, and it had not been spent already. It seems like so it doesn't appear to be legit; in any case, because electronic documents are effortlessly copied, banks were needed to beware of all e-money to ensure they hadn't been spent at this point.

## Twofold Spending issue

The twofold spending issue is the principle issue that should have been settled to present another electronic cash framework. The issue might have been settled by utilizing a focal confided-in outsider on the web, who could check that the electronic money has not been spent at this point.

Once upon a time, the thought was that this believed outsider could be in any way similar to a bank, specialist, or any element that can work with connections between different sides who both trust the outsider. But, unfortunately, there are a lot of disservices for confiding in outsiders; truth be told, in any monetary administrations.

In the 2008 monetary emergency when a few banks fizzled, it showed us there is nothing of the sort as a confided outsider. They bombed predominantly due to botch, or eagerness—or even numerous because of inclusion with unlawful bank exercises. Moreover, a big part of the grown-ups throughout the planet have no admittance to monetary administrations because monetary organizations are excessively far away or too costly to even consider utilizing. Outsiders are business substances; along these lines, they will charge expenses for their administrations.

On the off chance that you contemplate creating another electronic cash, one of your objectives ought to make it open to anybody throughout the planet. Outsiders can suspend clients' records. For instance, a couple of years prior, PayPal suspended the WikiLeaks gift account and froze its resources. In addition, PayPal guaranteed WikiLeaks urges others to participate in criminal behavior. This was not a consequence of a legitimate cycle, yet rather the aftereffect of dread of becoming undesirable with Washington. Outsiders can likewise deny or restrict admittance to your resources. For instance, in 2015 in Greece, the banks had restricted admittance for cash withdrawal due to the scramble for the banks.

On the off chance that you contemplate developing another electronic cash, one of your objectives ought to make it available to anybody throughout the planet. Outsiders can suspend clients' records. For instance, a couple of years prior, PayPal suspended the WikiLeaks gift account and froze its resources. In addition, PayPal guaranteed WikiLeaks urges others to participate in criminal behavior. This was not a consequence of legitimate interaction but instead the aftereffect of dread of becoming undesirable with Washington. Outsiders can likewise deny or restrict admittance to your resources. For instance, in 2015 in Greece, the banks had restricted admittance for cash withdrawal due to the scramble for the banks.

## Twofold spending arrangement

The answer for twofold spending without outsiders presently exists, which is what blockchain considered Bitcoin. Bitcoin was the principal application for the twofold spending issue without utilizing outsiders or any contribution with any brought-together framework. Satoshi Nakamoto thought of the possibility of Bitcoin and made its unique reference execution. Along these lines, Satoshi has tackled the twofold spending issue utilizing an innovation that is called today Blockchain Technology. The framework depends on cryptographic verification rather than trust. Blockchain innovation was initially utilized as cryptographic money for the installment exchange between two gatherings; however, these days, it very well may be utilized for some different administrations, for example:

- Notary Services,
- Identity administrations,
- Voting administrations, etc.

## The incomparable Ledger

The record is a kind of information base where affirmed exchanges are recorded. Conventional brought together record frameworks work fundamentally the same way as the Blockchain record framework; be that as it may, there are not many contrasts.

## Brought together record:

An old method of doing a record framework that a bank brings together. For instance, it works like this: on the off chance you buy from me, you pay me; truly, you would just start exchanging your financial balance to my ledger. Then, at that point, both of those banks, assuming they are not the equivalent, would have every body of the subtleties of the exchange enrolled. But, be that as it may, just those two banks would have the option to get to those exchange subtleties. Along these lines, no different banks nor any other individual would approach those subtleties.

Assuming somebody needs to approach see the subtleties, they need to ask the bank for approval first. Everything relies upon what is the justification behind the entrance. In any case, the point here is that this conventional record framework is as yet working similarly. There are a few various types of record frameworks; be that as it may, with regards to Blockchain's extraordinary record framework, it's not brought together. It dwells on the distributed organization; along these lines, it's a decentralized record framework.

**Disseminated Ledger:**

Blockchain stages don't utilize a brought-together information base; all things being equal, every hub has a duplicate of the record that dwells on the distributed organization. Cryptographic forms of money, like Bitcoin records, just store balance data in the disseminated record. Be that as it may, different stages can, truth be told, put away other data. Blockchain stages, for example, blockchain, can store any data in the disseminated record. A few models are:

- Identity data
- Patient data
- Real bequest data, and so forth

This technique is otherwise called a public record or permissionless record. When there is no focal authority overseeing admittance to the record, this record is known as a public record or, once more, a permissionless record. So fundamentally, you, or anybody, could join the current distributed organization (free of charge, obviously) and get a duplicate of the record of all current exchanges that have at any point been recorded on the blockchain. This would trace back to January of 2009, when the extraordinary record started to work interestingly. As should be obvious, this is something contrary to what the current financial frameworks are giving.

**Private Ledger**

When there is a focal authority overseeing admittance to the record, it's then, at that point, called a private record, otherwise called a permission record. Again, this is not a distributed organization, and you would need to request authorization from the focal server to approach a duplicate of the record.

The blockchain record is envisioned as a progression of squares that are associated with one another. Each square is made of a header containing metadata, such as its past block hash, Merkle root hash, and nonce, followed by a rundown of exchanges. Finally, the squares are associated with one another by referring to each of its folks' square hash.

**The Blocks**

All squares in the fundamental chain are numbered, beginning with the number 0, then, at that point, 1, 2, 3, 4, 5, etc. So the green square is the principal block that was made, and it's otherwise called a beginning square, and it has a square number zero.

The purple squares are the ones that are shaping short and invalid chains, and they are called blockchain forks. Blockchain forks do happen all the time. Furthermore, these side forks, otherwise called stranded forks.

A Bitcoin block is made at regular intervals, all things considered; be that as it may, Ethereum blocks are set up in like clockwork by and large. The square tallness is the number of squares in a chain, and the beginning square is short 1. Blocks on side forks can have similar square tallness as squares on the fundamental chain. Specific hubs on the distributed organization are making these squares. These hubs are called excavators. Every one of the excavators gathers each exchange that individuals are shipping off one another over the organization, and just substantial exchanges are transferred to different hubs. Every excavator takes some of these gathered activities and places them in a recently shaped square. These arrangements of exchanges are numbered tx0, tx1, tx2, …, etc. Tx represents exchange, trailed by the number. The principal exchange (tx0) is otherwise called the coinbase exchange. This is the exchange where the excavator relegates a square compensation to his location. This is how Bitcoins are made. For Bitcoin excavators, at this point in 2017, the square award is 12.5 Bitcoins; be that as it may, once upon a time of the beginning square, the prize was 50 bitcoins for each square creation. For Bitcoin, the square prize is divided after every 210,000 squares. Once there have been 64 halvings, the square award will be zero. There will be a most extreme number of 21 million Bitcoin available for use in the extended period of 2140. For example, other Bitcoin exchanges, tx1 or tx2, are the conventional exchange where the bitcoins are moved from the proprietor's address to a beneficiary location. Every exchange requires a little exchange expense. This expense will continue expanding as a motivating force for the excavators to make new squares because the square award will keep being brought down.

When the excavator has developed the square, he should address a hash puzzle applied on his rundown of exchanges. The excavator who initially addresses the hash puzzle is permitted to communicate his square on the distributed organization. The square also incorporates the riddle's answer, likewise called the nonce, in the square header. This is, obviously, accessible to any individual who needs to see it, and the subtleties for each square can be found at www.blockchain.info. Other excavators on the organization will get this square, and they approve it before attaching it to their chain of squares. It happens consistently that one more substantial square is communicated on the organization because another excavator has addressed the riddle almost simultaneously.

At the point when this occurs, impermanent forks are made. For instance, fork An and fork B. How about we expect that 70 % of the excavators on the organization are chipping away at fork A, and the remainder of the diggers are dealing with fork B. In this model, fork A becomes the fundamental chain since it comprises the longest series of squares from the beginning square. Therefore, excavators ought to consistently chip away at the longest chain. In this model, blocks on fork B will become stranded squares.

The excavator who addresses the hash puzzle, and his square is on the fundamental chain, will get the square prize and every one of the exchanges expenses (tx1 and tx2) in this square. On the other hand, the excavator who has addressed the hash puzzle, and his square is a vagrant fork, can't spend the square award and exchange expenses since his square isn't on the fundamental chain.

## Platform testing

Because of the scaling exchanges, the first blockchain that was made back in 2009 requires specific support. In earlier days, there were a number of exchanges; be that as it may, as of mid-2017, there are near 150,000 exchanges each day. That implies more than 6,250 exchanges inside 60 minutes, which boils down to 105 exchanges consistently, which means almost 2 exchanges occur each second.

I trust you can comprehend that the framework expects updates to ensure that a large number of exchanges can be taken care of by the organization. As of now, there are many blockchain occupations available, and on the off chance that you have great programming abilities, you could turn into an extraordinary blockchain engineer.

Blockchain engineers are generously compensated; here in the UK, an extremely durable blockchain designer pay rate begins from 80K to 150K, even 300K each year, and I am discussing pounds, not dollars. The issue is that a couple of individuals comprehend blockchain, as the information on detail required can be overpowering and unquestionably not the best thing in the world for everybody. Having a digit of information on C++, SQL, or Python could be exceptionally worthwhile, and it that you are into learning these programming dialects, it will pay off. Twenty years prior, everybody was on with IT as the future, and mastering such abilities will be required for most future positions. It is unquestionably great to have some IT foundation, particularly on the off chance you intend to turn into your bank; notwithstanding, how about briefly explaining. Mastering IT abilities can mean numerous things; you ought to be explicit and practice along these lines.

Without much of a stretch, I can say that the future positions that will take care of big-time are programming engineers, or to be more precise, Blockchain designers. Where to begin? Get an internet-based seminar on Python programming for fledglings, alongside a reference book. Nevertheless, before I start an entirely different subject on programming abilities, let me clarify a smidgen concerning what conditions current blockchain engineers are utilizing for testing purposes.

**Testnet**:

A testnet is an option blockchain utilized by engineers for testing purposes. The crypto coins mined on the testnet, otherwise called testnet coins, have no genuine worth. A testnet offers engineers a sandbox climate to analyze without utilizing the genuine crypto coins or agonizing over breaking the fundamental chain. The fundamental chain is additionally called the mainnet. On the off chance that you are pondering with regards to mining bitcoin, this is it. You can rapidly mine your Bitcoin or Ethereum test net coins by setting up your Bitcoin or Ethereum hub.

There are fewer excavators on the testnet, and the hash trouble is additionally sufficiently low to find arrangements more straightforward for addressing hash puzzles—also—getting a square prize. However, the mainnet and testnet are two individual organizations, and there is no accessibility to send coins starting with one stage then onto the next, nor the other way around. To chip away at the Bitcoin testnet, you want to produce a contrastingly organized testnet Bitcoin address. A Bitcoin testnet address consistently starts with the letter m or n. The Bitcoin testnet address doesn't chip away at the mainnet.

Be that as it may, with regards to Ethereum, there are no contrasts between testnet and mainnet. Nevertheless, a similar location will chip away at the two organizations: testnet also mainnet. Along these lines, you should be extremely mindful so as not to stir them up.

**Faucets:**

One more method for getting testnet coins is looking for a Bitcoin fixture or an Ethereum spigot. A fixture is a site that administers limited quantities of testnet coins on your location in return for following through with a responsibility portrayed by the site. You can, without much of a stretch, google search both: Bitcoin fixture and blockchain spigot.

# SegWit

As I just clarified some testing apparatuses for engineers, how about we see what else is out there that requires support regarding the genuine blockchain network. SegWit represents Segregated Witness. SegWit can be clarified in numerous ways. However, its specialized subtleties can be exceptionally confounding for a few; along these lines, I will attempt to clarify straightforwardly before truly plunging into it.

SegWit is a change on the blockchain network; explicitly, it's a change inside the squares. I'm an organization specialist, and it's not difficult to say that with regards to a choice of rolling out an improvement, particularly inside the creation climate, it is because there is a matter that should be tended to. The issue at present with the squares is straightforward. Each square can deal with 1MB of information, which means all exchange subtleties.

Once sufficient information is inside a square, the square gets fixed, and excavators begin to make another new square. The issue that should be attended to is that each square gets loaded up for certain information; however, without a doubt, it has been distinguished that there ought to be more information inside each square. I have clarified beforehand that each square contains bunches of information; truth be told, each exchange subtleties are recorded on the blockchain, explicitly inside the squares. The information recorded are the square number, objective location, source address, exchange esteem, hashing calculations, etc. The main datum recorded is the genuine content that contains the computerized marks and the general population keys. To have a square approved on the blockchain distributed organization, these pieces of the blockchain rules must be inside the content. Notwithstanding, it has been distinguished that the current circumstance is dialing back the framework, and a redesign is required. This scaling issue should have been tended to; along these lines, blockchain designers thought of a thought.

## Arrangement:

The arrangement is called SegWit. Be that as it may, the genuine arrangement to carry out SegWit is to eliminate the content from the squares, making the squares lighter; along these lines, leaving more space for extra exchanges also accelerate the framework. Be that as it may, the proposition has a potential incidental effect. The content is as yet going to be needed as the blockchain guidelines can't be changed; along these lines, some portion of the proposition is that there will likewise be a drawn-out block that will have the content. This is exceptionally confounding for some, particularly for individuals who have no specialized foundation. The other issue is that engineers don't know whether it will work out alright or not: even though they accept it is required, subsequently the change proposition in any case. We just can discover once carried out. This arrangement is an answer for some different issues as well. One is that every exchange charge is exceptionally modest; notwithstanding, it very well maybe even more affordable. You need to comprehend that bitcoin is magnificent computerized money with regards to qualities, for example, $100 worth or more. Be that as it may, to carry out it worldwide in each store requires a few overhauls.

For instance, assuming you make an installment utilizing Bitcoin valued at $100, the exchange expenses could cost you around $0.30 pennies. Notwithstanding, when you need to purchase a coffee from your neighborhood coffeehouse that costs a dollar, a $0.30 exchange charge could be simply excessively costly. Along these lines, what has been distinguished is this: If we could add more exchanges to each obstruct, similar to twice so much, that could imply that every exchange would cost half of what it is currently. Be that as it may, to fit more exchanges to a square, something must be eliminated. What has been found is that the content can be re-composed and added to a drawn-out block on the first square, and this would be called Segregated Witness, otherwise known as SegWit.

**For what reason is it called SegWit?**

The observer is otherwise called Cryptographic confirmations, and the marks that are utilized are additionally seeing the verifications. Isolating the marks from both the exchange information structure and the square information structure into their information structure. Removing the marks from the exchange information structure is the fundamental explanation; be that as it may, there are some incidental effects, so how about we investigate them. In the first place, incidental effects are not in every case terrible; truth be told, in respect to SegWit, there are some exceptionally certain results conceivable.

The first objective was to tidy up a portion of the elements of Bitcoin. One thing that isn't static inside the exchange information is the computerized signature. To be reasonable, all the other things covered by the mark, along these lines, can't be changed successfully, except if discrediting the mark; be that as it may, the actual mark can be malleated. Along these lines, when the mark would be removed from the exchange information, the exchange ID would no longer be found on the mark.

The exchange ID's hash did not depend on the mark, implying that the exchange ID can't be malleated. This, in itself, is a monstrous turn of events. On the other hand, it assists with anchoring exchanges, lightning organizations, and installment channels. It will settle bunches of issues that we at present have with exchange flexibility.

**Exchange flexibility:**

In straightforward terms, exchange flexibility is a stopper in Bitcoin, and other cryptographic frameworks, where you can roll out unapproved improvements to exchanges and once again broadcast with an alternate exchange ID. But, of course, you can't change where the assets are coming from, nor where the assets are going, because the mark covers that; notwithstanding, you can make little alterations to the mark.

How about we think about this in straightforward terms. Suppose that the mark contained the number 5. The investigation of the calculations 5 and 05 are very similar, however assuming you cushion a number with a particular goal in mind, it will change the unique finger impression of that exchange, regardless of whether that mark is deciphered the same way. Along these lines, you can change part of the mark since it does not cover them, and they would deliver an exchange with an altogether unique ID. By doing that, you can stick it into the organization and create turmoil. Exchange flexibility has been faulted for certain burglaries and Bitcoin trades, where individuals, for the most part, are getting a type of twofold pull-out, utilizing exchange pliability. It additionally permits you to complete a DOS – Denial of Service Attack, against the organization; also against individuals who are utilizing installment channels or fastening numerous exchanges together.

**How does SegWit permit more exchanges in the organization?**

One of the fascinating symptoms of SegWit is that you can begin counting block estimates contrastingly and give some ability to increment straightforwardly through the SegWit. Exchanges are the way to get into the blockchain; along these lines, you want a mark on the exchange to be approved to the blockchain. Notwithstanding, when the exchange is in the blockchain, no one checks those marks at any point in the future; ordinarily, we don't return to see old exchanges that happened quite sometime in the past. They're just covered inside the blockchain. They have been approved: along these lines, old exchanges are as of now trusted. The mark is just utilized once for approval. For instance, when you compose a paper check, you have the choice to go to your web-based financial framework and take a gander at the picture of the check after it has been submitted and gotten the money for. It's not a piece of the bank articulation, and you needn't bother with it for something besides to check it once to see that it was approved; after, it's just sticking around, no requirement for it any longer. The same thing applies to marks. You need to comprehend that computerized marks take 75% of the complete space of certain exchanges. Furthermore, the more exchanges there are, the greater the mark gets. Enormous, complex contents and multi marks have tremendous marks, and they occupy a great deal of room on the blockchain, and, again, no one at any point thinks often about them whenever they have been approved.

The other piece of the SegWit wasn't considered long ago because fixing flexibility and eliminating exchange marks from the exchange information requires thinking about the entire organization. It's been accepted that it needs a hard fork. Nevertheless, there is the best approach utilizing a delicate fork rather than a hard fork. Without a doubt, it's an interesting stunt. This technique permits you to put an adaptation number before the Bitcoin script. What that does, is permits you to overhaul the adaptation number of the content, while old customers can't see the distinction, yet at the same time ready to approve exchanges altogether. Previous clients can keep on working without redesigning, and all that is distinctive in that they are underwriting somewhat less than they previously did. Furthermore, new customers can overhaul scripts when you have another adaptation of content (this is magnificent). You can present unlimited measures of delicate forks corresponding to changing a wide range of prearranging instruments. This stunt isn't simply great to use for SegWit, however any remaining sorts of new turns of events. This is speeding up the development of the prearranging language. Through and through these perspectives: Segregated observer, Transaction flexibility, expanding the limit of the square by eliminating bunches of data that is not utilized after approval, and a similar time overhauling adaptation scripts—make a genuinely convincing component and resolve loads of issues.

## Soft fork VS Hard fork

As a matter of importance, let me clarify a little with regards to delicate fork initiation. A democratic interaction generally finishes it. Yet, another advancement is called Version Bits, otherwise called BIP 9, which was presented in equal and permitted you to have different delicate forks.

It permits you to assume a specific piece in the adaptation of the square set, which means you need to carry out this delicate fork; the excavators then, at that point, set that piece. Once 75% of the squares have that piece set, you are initiating the component; then, at that point, once 95% of the squares have the piece set, then that features.

It's a two-venture casting a ballot interaction.
It has been done on different events, like Check Lock Time Verify. These gradual highlights can be decided on equal. Beforehand, they had been carried out by expanding the squares and by overhauling block adaptation. For model, refreshing square form 3 to obstruct adaptation 4, etc.
Nevertheless, presently, you can transform the square form into a square field; in this manner, you can do every one of these equations. Beforehand, it

was that just one delicate fork might have been carried out at that point, and the vote must be finished coincidentally. It is difficult to acknowledge one, excuse another, and move to the following. Be that as it may, with the new proposition, you can carry out different delicate forks simultaneously.

The significant component of the delicate fork is that it's forward viable. In straightforward terms, let me give a guide to better arrangements. First, envision that you need to open an old Microsoft word archive. Word 1998 archives can be opened with the current adaptation of Microsoft Word. This is the thing that retrogressive similarity is, which means it perceives old configurations.

Then again, the forward similarity is the point at which the adaptation of Microsoft Word from 1998 that has not been redesigned would, in any case, open an archive that we use today, or if nothing else, with a particular goal in mind. It will most likely be unable to see all unique subtleties effectively and will most likely be unable to see a portion of the highlights; be that as it may, it actually would have the option to open the archive. Along these lines, delicate forks have forward similarity, implying that customers who have not yet moved up to the new code won't break and will not quit approving, so they can, in any case, keep up with approving on the current agreement chain. All there is that they are approving fewer data since they will most likely be unable to see the new highlights; notwithstanding, they can disregard them while approving.

The hard fork, by examination, implies that assuming you don't redesign, you can at this point don't endorse squares, and you are at this point don't some portion of the agreement chain, along these lines, in case you don't overhaul, you are not on the organization.

**Conquering hazards:**

There are consistent changes, particularly when taking a gander at similarities. As I referenced previously, any change to the framework obviously will cause impacts. Delicate forks, hard forks, they all have bugs, even though many highlights are constantly tried on Testnet. For instance, an isolated observer testnet ran for a long time before execution, which permits more confidence before any change. Excavators have become exceptionally worried about any change and ensuring there are different tests before any execution happens. The overall conviction is that delicate forks are less hazardous than hard forks. However, certain individuals distinguish the issue that they don't constrain the organization to overhaul, which means you can wind up with bunches of old customers that approve fewer exchanges. Notwithstanding, some different designers like to have to a greater extent, a severe methodology and simply trust that assuming you don't redesign, you ought to be off the organization. Along these lines, it's more similar to a philosophical issue rather than specialized.

**Lightning Network**

Lightning network is a Layer 2 organization, otherwise called Data Layer organization. It expects to scale distributed organizations from millions to billions of exchanges each second while utilizing brilliant agreements. For instance, getting compensated not month to month nor week after week, but rather consistently. Refreshing, isn't that so? I'm certain you would cherish that as well! Envision checking your internet-based compensation slip and seeing it continually changing, showing you an alternate sum each second. On the whole, why don't we take a look at why the thought was brought into the world in any case.

## Exchanges are slow

Getting installments month to month is ludicrous. I used to get compensated week after week prior, which is significantly better; notwithstanding, I've also had many positions before where I used to get compensated day by day. Getting compensated day by day is what I generally preferred; notwithstanding, I was on a money-to-hand premise, and it was not recorded anyplace; along these lines, I can't represent those days. Utilizing blockchain, particularly lighting organization, can permit you to get approved installment simultaneously, which is enlisted in the extraordinary record until the end of time.

As a representative, I accept it's a great method for getting compensated; be that as it may, think according to a business perspective. Envision that you have an organization that utilizes a large number of individuals. Every month individuals are chipping away at payslips, ensuring everybody will get compensated effectively. Still, before any approval, it needs to go through the bank, truth be told, many banks, to get everybody paid. Along these lines, lightning organizations will be the top choice of each business.

Since you have a piece of decent information on how blockchain and Bitcoin function with regards to lightning organizations, it's twisting the principles a smidgen; allow me to clarify why: we realize that when we send a Bitcoin, we broadcast the exchange, then, at that point, we need to hang tight for affirmation, and affirmations are just showing up at regular intervals as a square.

When the square has been made, it bunches numerous exchanges, getting enrolled on the record. Notwithstanding, assuming you are sitting tight for the following affirmation, you need to trust that the following square will be approved, which may require an additional 10 minutes. Since a lightning network chips away at the top of the current framework, utilizing an alternate layer has its layer for moment installment.

## Exchanges are costly

The Lightning network guarantees no expenses on the exchanges. Once more, this is new, essentially because every exchange has expenses that occasionally are significantly bigger than the past exchanges were. Expenses are for focusing on your exchanges inside the rundown of different exchanges. The more expenses you would pay, the quicker you would get the affirmations. Paying no expenses seems like you are potentially never going to get affirmed by the organization.

## Arrangement

You should consider it in straightforward terms. Envision when you go to a Pub where the server lets you know that you need to pay cash, or on the other hand, assuming you decide to pay with a card, the base request needs to reach $5. This is because, for every exchange, the bar needs to pay a specific expense to the supplier. Notwithstanding, assuming you open a tab and pay just a single time, eventually, there will be a single exchange expense that requires installment.

When you make an installment channel on the lightning organization, you need to store a specific measure of bitcoin. Presently you are demonstrating proprietorships for those bitcoins by giving them over to the organization. It additionally works with multi-marks. The framework has a method of implementing these arrangements of rules; in this manner, you don't need to trust that the square will be affirmed. When the exchange has been declared, it's is prompt; consequently, you don't need to delay until these assets are supported.

As we don't constrain the excavators to compose these exchanges on the blockchain, as ordinarily, you would need to pay the diggers for exchange expenses. This framework permits you to make numerous installments; be that as it may, you possibly need to communicate it when it's fundamental. At the current phase of August 2017, we realize that the idea works; notwithstanding, this product is a work in progress. It is exceptionally convoluted to carry out, along these lines, and it is going to take some time. Any bug in the code can cause an explosive result; along these lines, there is certifiably not a completely working goal yet.

# Blockchain Advantages and Disadvantages

Most blockchains are planned as a decentralized information base that capacities as a disseminated computerized record—this blockchain records and stores information in blocks coordinated in a sequential arrangement and connected through cryptographic verifications. The production of blockchain innovation raised many benefits in an assortment of enterprises, giving expanded security in trustless conditions. Be that as it may, its decentralized nature additionally brings a few inconveniences. For example, when contrasted with conventional brought-together information bases, blockchains present restricted effectiveness and require an expanded capacity limit.

## Advantages

### Distributed

Since blockchain information is frequently put away in a large number of gadgets on a disseminated organization of hubs, the framework and the information are exceptionally impervious to specialized disappointments and vindictive assaults. Moreover, each organization hub can reproduce and store a duplicate of the information base. Along these lines, there is no weak link: a solitary hub going disconnected doesn't influence the accessibility or security of the organization.

Interestingly, numerous traditional information bases depend on a solitary or a couple of servers and are more defenseless against specialized disappointments and digital assaults.

### Dependability

Affirmed blocks will probably not be turned around, implying that whenever information has been enlisted into the blockchain, it is incredibly hard to eliminate or transform it. This makes blockchain an extraordinary innovation for putting away monetary records or whatever other information where a review trail is required because each change is followed and for all time recorded on a disseminated and public record.

For instance, a business could utilize blockchain innovation to keep deceitful conduct from its representatives. In this situation, the blockchain could give a protected and stable record of all monetary exchanges inside the organization. This would make it harder for a representative to conceal dubious exchanges.

### Distrustful framework

In most conventional installment frameworks, exchanges rely upon the two gatherings included, yet additionally on a middle person - like a bank, charge card organization, or installment supplier. However, when utilizing blockchain innovation, this is excessive because the appropriated organization of hubs confirms the exchanges through an interaction known as mining. Consequently, Blockchain is frequently alluded to as a 'trustless' framework.

Along these lines, a blockchain framework invalidates the danger of confiding in a solitary association and diminishes the general expenses and exchange charges by removing middle people and outsiders.

### Disadvantages

### 51% Attacks

The Proof of Work agreement calculation that secures the Bitcoin blockchain has demonstrated to be exceptionally proficient throughout the long term. Notwithstanding, a couple of potential assaults can be performed against blockchain networks, and 51% of assaults are among the most talked about. Such an assault might occur on the off chance that one substance figures out how to control over half of the organization's hashing power, which would ultimately permit them to disturb the organization by deliberately barring or adjusting the requesting of exchanges.

Notwithstanding being hypothetically conceivable, there was never an effective 51% assault on the Bitcoin blockchain. As the organization becomes bigger, the security increments. It is very far-fetched that excavators will put away a lot of cash and assets to assault Bitcoin as they are better compensated for acting truly. Other than that, an effective 51% assault would simply have the option to adjust the latest exchanges for a brief timeframe because squares are connected through cryptographic confirmations (changing more established squares would require theoretical degrees of registering power). Additionally, the Bitcoin blockchain is exceptionally versatile and would rapidly adjust as a reaction to an assault.

**Information modification**

One more disadvantage of blockchain frameworks is that it is undeniably challenging to adjust them whenever information has been added to the blockchain. While dependability is one of blockchain's benefits, it isn't, in every case, great. Changing blockchain information or code is generally exceptionally requesting and frequently requires a hard fork, where one chain is deserted and another one is taken up.

**Private keys**

Blockchain utilizes public-key (or hilter kilter) cryptography to give clients responsibility for digital currency units (or some other blockchain information). Each blockchain address has a comparing private key. While the location can be shared, the private key ought to be kept a mystery. Clients need their private key to get to their assets, implying that they go about their bank. If a client loses their private key, the cash is successfully lost, and there is no way around it.

## Inefficient

Blockchains, particularly those utilizing Proof of Work, are exceptionally wasteful. Since mining is exceptionally aggressive and there is only one victor at regular intervals, crafted by every other excavator is squandered. As excavators are consistently attempting to expand their computational power, so they have a more noteworthy shot at observing a substantial square hash, the assets utilized by the Bitcoin network has expanded fundamentally over a recent couple of years, and it at present burns through more energy than numerous nations, like Denmark, Ireland, and Nigeria.

## Capacity

Blockchain records can develop exceptionally enormously after some time—the Bitcoin blockchain at present needs around 200 GB of capacity. However, the current development in blockchain size gives off an impression of being overwhelming the development in hard drives and the organization hazards losing hubs on the off chance that the record turns out to be excessively enormous for people to download and store.

## How Blockchain Can Power Up Your Business

Cryptographic forms of money are not the only things that can be traded on blockchains. Through its appropriated and decentralized nature, this innovation has a number of benefits that can be beneficial to organizations in a diverse range of enterprises:

## #1 Better Transparency

One of the most remarkable characteristics of blockchain is the ability to view and examine its exchange records for public locations. Financial frameworks and businesses are therefore tasked with acting sincerely towards their clients, the local community, and the organization's development.

## #2 Increased Efficiency

Due to its decentralized nature, Blockchain takes the place of go-betweens, for example, in the installment and land fields. In contrast with conventional monetary administrations, blockchain works with quicker exchanges by permitting P2P cross-line moves with computerized money. In addition, the executive's processes are made more proficient with a brought together arrangement of proprietorship records and brilliant agreements that would computerize inhabitant landowner arrangements.

## #3 Better Security

Blockchain is safer than other recordkeeping frameworks because each new exchange is scrambled and connected to the one-time exchange. As its name implies, a blockchain is composed of computer systems meeting up to agree on a 'block'; this square is then added to a record, which forms a 'chain.' Blockchain is framed by a convoluted line of numerical numbers and is difficult to be modified once shaped. This changeless and morally sound nature of blockchain makes it protected from misrepresented data and hacks. Its decentralized nature additionally provides it with an extraordinary nature of being 'trustless' – gatherings can work securely without having to depend on trust.

## #4 Improved Traceability

With the blockchain record, each time trade of merchandise is recorded on a Blockchain, and a review trail is available to follow where the products came from. This can not just assist with further developing security and forestall misrepresentation in return related organizations. However, it can likewise assist with confirming the genuineness of the exchanged resources. In enterprises like medication, it very well may be utilized to follow the production network from producer to distributer, or in the craftsmanship business to give an unquestionable confirmation of proprietorship.

## Blockchain-as-a-Service for Simpler Integration

The issue that numerous organizations face is that blockchain is refined to incorporate and come up short on a specialized group that is knowledgeable in this field. BaaS or Blockchain-as-a-Service organizations permit clients to incorporate Blockchain innovation into their organizations effectively, without interruption to their day-by-day processes. One such organization that distinguished the requirement for BaaS is Broctagon Fintech Group.

With a worldwide presence across 7 nations, Broctagon gives chief fintech arrangements, including multi-resource liquidity, financier innovation arrangements, and blockchain improvement. Organizations are additionally uncertain about blockchain reconciliation, particularly about putting enormous amounts of assets into improvement for an innovation that is as yet considered 'troublesome.' Starter units like Blockchain-in-a-Box permits present-day organizations to make a proof-of-idea to affirm blockchain's reasonability and attainability for their business before setting out on a complete turn of events. Financial backers are almost certain to fund an undertaking they can see, rather than simply a theoretical thought. With its Blockchain-in-a-Box starter unit, organizations can make a completely unmistakable stage to hang out in their market and gain certainty for their undertakings.

Blockchain has the potential for some utilization cases appropriate to many enterprises, and BaaS works with that development from 'problematic' into 'standard.'

**What are the benefits of blockchain innovation for organizations?**

The fundamental benefits of Blockchain innovation are decentralization, unchanging nature, security, and straightforwardness.

Blockchain innovation takes into consideration confirmation without hosting to be reliant upon third-gatherings.

- The information structure in a blockchain is attached, as it were. Along these lines, the information can't be modified or erased.
- It utilizes ensured cryptography to get the information records. Additionally, the current record is reliant upon its neighboring finished square to finish the cryptography interaction.
- Every one of the exchanges and information is connected to the square after the most extreme trust confirmation. There is an agreement of all the record members on what is to be recorded in the square.
- The exchanges are recorded in sequential requests. Along these lines, every one of the squares in the blockchain is time stepped.
- The record is disseminated across every hub in the blockchain who are the members. So along these lines, it is disseminated.
- The exchanges put away in the squares are contained in many PCs taking an interest in the chain. Consequently, it is decentralized. There is no likelihood that the information assuming lost can't be recuperated.
- The exchanges that happen are straightforward. The people who are given authority can see the exchange.
- The beginning of any record can be followed along the chain to its starting place.
- Since different agreement conventions are expected to approve the

passage, it eliminates the danger of copy section or misrepresentation.

- With the brilliant agreements, the organizations can pre-set conditions on the blockchain. Then, the programmed exchanges are set off just when the conditions are met.

Precautionary measures when organizations put resources into the blockchain innovation:

- All organizations that are keen to put resources into blockchain innovation should initially play out an essential assessment to check whether it is genuinely attainable for their plan of action. Many organizations may not see a profit from their interests in the underlying years. Any unstructured execution of the blockchain innovation might prompt vital disappointments. Along these lines, organizations are encouraged to perform granular evaluations at the utilization case level to figure out which application can be instigated with blockchain innovation. The focuses where it may be applied must be distinguished, and its effect must be evaluated with explicit use cases. The right essential methodology is the thing that is expected to use the most extreme advantages of blockchain innovation.

**Enterprises where blockchain innovation can be applied:**

Blockchain innovation can be applied to any industry. Agribusiness, banking, medical services, instruction, web-based business, property, mining, retail, transport and coordinations, media and diversion, auto the rundown continues. An exhaustive comprehension of its execution will yield the regions where it very well may be applied and how.

**Blockchain engineering for Businesses:**

Blockchain engineering incorporates the general population and private choices. In the public choice, anybody can join and peruse. The blockchain in the general population can be made secure by allowing just approved members to compose. In a private-based blockchain proprietorship model, just approved members can join and peruse. Here additionally, the composing choice can again be apportioned to a couple. The kind of blockchain engineering will rely upon the business type and the region where it will be carried out.

**How might organizations exploit blockchain innovation?**

Since we know the advantages of blockchain innovation, let us perceive how it can help organizations. Blockchain innovation is, for the most part, used to store records and exchanges. The record might contain static or exchange-capable data.

**1. Static library:**

Here the record includes records that are put away as a reference of perspective reason. Take, for example, the land title. There are many instances of equivocalness in title proprietorship. With blockchain innovation, the records once put away can't be modified. Any progressions are time-stepped. If there should emerge an incident of the question, the title can be followed through the beginning. Different spots where it may be utilized are in-licenses, research articles, food handling, and beginning records.

**2. Personality:**

This is like the static library. Nevertheless, this structures a different case because of the personality-related data put away. The fragments that may be utilized very well are for personality cheats, casting a ballot, common library, police records, and legal disputes.

## 3. Brilliant agreements:

Here, many pre-characterized conditions must be met on the off chance that the exchange needs to get approved. The activities are then set into motion once the conditions are met. Say, for instance, in the protection guarantee payout. First, the protection supplier can set the conditions to be met for protection claims. In this case, the purchaser's cases must meet the agreement's conditions for the sum to be moved. Different regions where it very well may be carried out are music discharges, cash-value exchanging, etc.

## 4. Dynamic library:

The record for this situation continues to refresh as merchandise/administrations are traded on the computerized stage. The best-utilized case is in a medication production network. The inventory of medications directly from the producer to the wholesaler finally to the pharmacy can be intended. The updates give data on the progress of medications, and this can be used to stop the inventory of fake medications on the lookout.

## 5. Installment library:

This is a powerful library that updates as the money, or digital currency installments are made on the organization. This is beneficial for worldwide installments in business.

# The Capability Of Blockchain

Subtleties on the capability of blockchain, its suggestions for evaluators, how the accounts can lead, and what abilities are fundamental for what's to come.

## Blockchain and the eventual fate of accounts

Tech Faculty's report on Blockchain portrays the innovation and its probably sway on business, specifically on the accounts.

Blockchain is a recording innovation. It is worried about the exchange of responsibility for and keeping a record of precise monetary data. The accounts calling is comprehensively worried about the estimation and correspondence of monetary data and the investigation of said data. A significant part of the calling is worried about discovering or estimating privileges and commitments over property or arranging how to best distribute monetary assets. For accountants, utilizing blockchain gives clearness over responsibility for and presence of commitments and could significantly further develop effectiveness.

Blockchain can improve the accounts by diminishing the expenses of keeping up with and accommodating records and giving outright conviction over the proprietorship and history of resources. In addition, blockchain could assist accountants with acquiring clearness over the accessible assets and commitments of their associations and let loose assets focus on arranging and valuation rather than recordkeeping.

Close by other computerization patterns, and for example, AI, blockchain will prompt increasingly more value-based level accounts being done – however, not by accountants. All things being equal, effective accountants will work on evaluating the genuine financial understanding of blockchain records, wedding the record to monetary reality, and valuation. For instance, blockchain may make the presence of an indebted person certain. However, its recoverable worth and financial worth are as yet debatable. What's more, a resource's proprietorship may be unquestionable by blockchain records. However, its condition, area, and genuine worth will, in any case, should be guaranteed.

By dispensing with compromises and giving conviction over exchange history, blockchain could likewise consider expansions in the extent of accounts, bringing more regions into the thought that are considered excessively troublesome or temperamental to quantify, for example, the worth of the information that an organization holds.

Blockchain is a substitution for accounting and compromise work. This could compromise crafted by accountants in those spaces while adding solidarity to those zeroed in on offering some incentive somewhere else. For instance, in due diligence in consolidations and acquisitions, appropriated agreement throughout key figures permits more opportunity to be spent on judgemental regions and appeal, and a generally speaking quicker process.

**Implications of blockchain for inspectors**

Blockchain has applications in outside review. For example, performing affirmations of an organization's monetary status would be less fundamental, assuming a few or every one of the exchanges that underlie that status is noticeable on blockchains. This proposition would mean a significant change in the manner that reviews work.

When joined with suitable information investigation, a blockchain arrangement could assist with the conditional level affirmations associated with a review, and the evaluator's abilities would be better spent thinking about more significant level inquiries.

For instance, inspecting isn't simply checking the detail of whom an exchange was between and the money-related sum, yet additionally how it is recorded and characterized. On the off chance that an exchange credits cash, is this outpouring because of the cost of deals or expenses, or is it paying a loan boss or making a resource?

These judgemental components frequently require a setting that isn't accessible to the overall population; however, they rather require information on the business. With blockchain set up, the inspector will have more opportunities to zero in on these inquiries.

## How the calling can lead with blockchain

The transition to a monetary framework with a critical blockchain component offers numerous chances for the accounts. Accountants are viewed as specialists in record keeping, utilization of mind-boggling rules, business rationale, and principles set. They have the chance to guide and impact how blockchain is installed and utilized later on and to create blockchain-drove arrangements and administrations.

Blockchain should be created, normalized, and streamlined to turn out to be genuinely an indispensable piece of the monetary framework. This interaction is probably going to require numerous years – it has effectively been a long time since bitcoin started working, and there is a lot of work still to be finished. There are numerous blockchain applications and new businesses in this field. However, there are not very many that are past the confirmation of idea or pilot concentrate on stage. Accountants are taking an interest in the exploration. However, there is more for the calling to do. Creating guidelines and principles to cover blockchain will be no little test, and driving accounts firms and bodies can carry their aptitude to that work.

Accountants can likewise function as consultants to organizations considering joining blockchains themselves, giving exhortation on gauging the expenses and benefits of the new framework. accountants blend of business and monetary nous will situate them as key consultants to organizations moving toward these new advancements searching for a promising circumstance.

**Abilities for what's to come**

The pieces of accounts worried about conditional confirmation and completing the exchange of property privileges will be changed by blockchain, and brilliant agreement draws near.

The decrease in the requirement for compromise and question the executives joined with the expanded conviction around privileges and commitments will permit a more noteworthy spotlight on the most proficient method to represent and think about the exchanges and empower development in what regions can be represented. In addition, numerous current-day accounts division cycles can be streamlined through blockchain and other present-day advancements, for example, information investigation or AI; this will expand the effectiveness and worth of the accounts capacity.

Because of the abovementioned, the range of abilities addressed in accounts will change. Compromises and provenance verification, for example, will be diminished or discarded, while other areas such as innovation, warning, and other valuable exercises will expand. An evaluator's focus will need to change in order to properly examine an organization with critical blockchain-based exchanges. A confirmation of blockchain exchanges' precision or presence with outside sources is relatively unnecessary. However, there is still a lot of thoughtfulness regarding how those exchanges are recorded and perceived in the budget summaries and how judgemental components, for example, valuations, are chosen. In the long run, many transactions could be stored on blockchains, and evaluators and controllers would have the option of understanding the provenance of transactions progressively and confidently.

It is unlikely that accountants will have detail-by-detail knowledge of how blockchain works. Regardless, they need to recognize how to promote blockchain acceptance as well as consider its impact on their companies and customers. Additionally, they should be able to decide whether to move forward with an extension after consulting with both technologists and business partners. Finally, accountants abilities should extend to incorporate comprehension of the guideline highlights and elements of blockchain. ICAEW's ACA capability prospectus, for example, mentions blockchain.

## Blockchain and its potential impact on auditing and assurance

A few distributions have indicated that blockchain innovation may wipe out the requirement for a budget report review by a CPA reviewer by and large. If all exchanges are caught in an unchanging blockchain, then, at that point, what is left for a CPA reviewer to review?

While confirming the event of an exchange is a structure block in a budget summary review, it is only one of the significant angles. A review includes an appraisal that recorded exchanges are upheld by applicable proof, solid, unbiased, precise, and evident. The acknowledgment of an exchange into a solid blockchain may comprise adequate proper review proof for specific fiscal report statements like the exchange event (e.g., that a resource recorded on the blockchain has moved from a vendor to a purchaser). For instance, in a bitcoin exchange for an item, the Bitcoin exchange is recorded on the blockchain. In any case, the inspector could conceivably have the option to decide the item that was conveyed by exclusively assessing data on the

Bitcoin blockchain. Along these lines, recording an exchange in a blockchain might give adequate proper review proof identified with the idea of the exchange. An exchange recorded in a blockchain may, in any case, be:

- Unapproved, deceitful, or illicit
- Executed between related gatherings
- Connected to a side understanding that is "off-chain."
- Inaccurately characterized in the fiscal summaries.

Moreover, numerous exchanges recorded in the fiscal reports reflect assessed values that contrast with verifiable expenses. Auditors will, in any case, have to consider and perform review strategies on administration's appraisals, regardless of whether the fundamental exchanges are recorded in a blockchain.

Boundless blockchain reception might empower focal areas to acquire review information, and CPA auditors might foster strategies to get review proof straightforwardly from blockchains. Notwithstanding, in any event, for such exchanges, the CPA reviewer needs to consider the danger that the data is erroneous because of mistake or extortion. This will introduce new difficulties because a blockchain likely would not be constrained by the element being evaluated. Therefore, the CPA reviewer should extricate the information from the blockchain and consider whether it is solid. This cycle might incorporate considering general data innovation controls (GITCs) identified with the blockchain climate. It additionally may require the CPA inspector to comprehend and evaluate the dependability of the agreement convention for the particular blockchain. This evaluation might have to incorporate the thought of whether the convention could be controlled.

As an ever-increasing number of associations investigate the utilization of private or public blockchains, CPA auditors should know about the potential effect this might have on their reviews as another wellspring of data for the fiscal summaries. They will likewise have to assess the executives' accounts arrangements for advanced resources and liabilities, which are at present not straightforwardly tended to in worldwide monetary revealing norms or US proper accounting rules. Finally, they should think about how to fit review techniques to exploit blockchain benefits to address steady dangers.

**Is the blockchain review trail in our not-so-distant future?**

There are numerous questions regarding how blockchain will affect the review and confirmation calls, incorporating the speed with which it will do as such. Blockchain is, as of now, affecting CPA auditors of those associations utilizing blockchain to record exchanges, and the pace of reception is relied upon to keep on expanding. In any case, blockchain innovation won't supplant monetary revealing and fiscal summary inspecting in the short term. Fiscal summaries reflect the executive's statements, including gauges, large numbers of which can't be effortlessly summed up or determined in a blockchain.

Besides, an autonomous review of fiscal reports improves the trust that is essential for the powerful working of the capital business sectors framework. Any disintegration of this trust might harm a substance's standing, stock cost, and investor esteem and can bring about fines, punishments, or loss of resources. Clients of fiscal summaries anticipate that CPA auditors should play out a free review of the budget reports utilizing their expert doubt. CPA auditors finish up whether they have gotten sensible affirmation that the fiscal summaries of an element, taken in general, are liberated from material misquote, regardless of whether because of extortion or blunder. A blockchain is probably not going to supplant these decisions by a fiscal summary reviewer.

CPA auditors need to screen advancements in blockchain innovation—it will affect customers' data innovation frameworks. Therefore, CPA auditors should be acquainted with the fundamentals of blockchain innovation and work with specialists to review the intricate specialized dangers related to blockchain.

What's more, CPA auditors ought to know about freedoms to use their customers' reception of blockchain innovation to further develop information gathering during the review. They ought to likewise consider whether blockchain innovation will permit them to make robotized review schedules. The evaluating calling should embrace and "incline in" to the chances and difficulties from inescapable blockchain reception. CPA auditors and confirmation suppliers are urged to screen improvements in blockchain innovation since they have a chance to develop, learn, and benefit from their all-around demonstrated capacity to adjust to the requirements of a quickly changing business world.

# Conclusion

I trust that you have gotten a handle on a tad bit of what the blockchain ascribes are and how complex the framework is. I will compose another book in a matter of seconds and clarify Bitcoin in more profundity and how to contribute safely and securely.

In general, what you need to comprehend is that blockchain and Bitcoin are not the same things. Blockchain is an innovation, and its first application was on the stage named Bitcoin. Bitcoin is blockchain. Nonetheless, Bitcoin itself is just a cryptocurrency that is fit for supplanting government-issued types of money. Not that many individuals will like the thought from the beginning. Blockchain has tackled the issue we have consistently confronted: trust, utilizing Elliptic Curve Cryptography, and an enormous measure of calculation power. Utilizing blockchain innovation empowers us to abstain from believing outsider administrations by supplanting them with advanced marks and numerical calculations. In this manner, any installment or trade over the web will be between 2 gatherings in particular. This is progressive as we can grow the trust hole, and the market of things to come not exclusively will be quicker and less expensive. However, it will have no constraints, like age, race, sex, occupation, ethnicity, or anything like that.

Assuming you tell your companion, who has never known about blockchain and feels that the individual isn't impacted, attempt to clarify that the blockchain impacts everybody:

- Person to Person
- Business to Business - B2B
- Machine to Machine - M2M

Even though blockchain won't assume control over the world, starting with one day then onto the next, it may require 10 years or two. Notwithstanding, everybody is impacted.

Blockchain is otherwise called the fate of cash; even though streaming cash sounds strange to a few, it not exclusively will occur. However, it has started almost 10 years, and won't stop, particularly utilizing another Lightning Network convention. Information insurance utilizing blockchain will be exceptionally getting and consistently give reality; utilizing a completely decentralized shared organization, information will consistently be accessible.

Since this high innovation empowers us to turn into our investors.

There is no need to have banks any longer later on; still, since we need to pay special mind to what we have, certain IT abilities will assist us with being more secure from digital hoodlums. When you see how simple it is to guard your web assets, you will also understand that it is significantly simpler than opening a ledger.

In this way, the progressions for the youthful and the cutting edge will accelerate the most common way of finding out about the crypto world. On the other hand, certain individuals might need to become familiar with the most difficult way possible, as many individuals have been hacked solely after starting to put resources into learning and executing security. The hour of Blockchain has started, and it will change the world.

Normal individuals with no specialized foundation might have a hard time believing it and most likely say that blockchain itself isn't fit for anything. Be that as it may, programming engineers, security specialists, enormous monetary organizations, FinTech new businesses, and banks, as of now, have paid a distinct fascination, just as they have contributed and made their conventions. Intel, Microsoft, Cisco Systems, Dell, and many more huge, top-of-the-line innovation firms, are now all around the blockchain and its little complexities. Hence, the days are building up to arrive at the enormous detonation of the change, the innovation of things to come, or, I should say, the following web!

Much thanks to you for buying this book. I trust this title has given a few bits of knowledge into what is truly in the background regarding the fate of cash and carrying on with Work either with individuals or machines. While I have intended to keep away from a substantial number of technical terms that can be expected under the circumstances regarding how the Blockchain functions, this is a high-level guide, and a few occurrences were only difficult to do as such. My impending book on Bitcoin will give more subtleties on the most proficient method to put resources into advanced gold securely and safely.

Furthermore, I will address Cryptocurrency exchanging and how to perceive the perfect opportunity to put resources into Bitcoin or some other Cryptocurrency. I will likewise give direction on how you can turn into a digger by leasing hardware, too, how you can begin mining advanced cash utilizing your PC or even your Android telephone.

In conclusion, assuming you partook in the book, kindly set aside some effort to share your musings and post an audit. It would be exceptionally valued!